SERVING IN HOSTILE PLACES VOLUME TWO

Setting Up Member Care in Hazardous Contexts

HAMILTON T. BURKE, PH.D.

Effective Kingdom Service in Hostile Places:
Advanced Training and Support for International workers
and the Organizations that send them

Vol 2. Setting Up Member Care in Hazardous Contexts

By Hamilton T. Burke, Ph.D.

The information presented in this book is derived from the author's 30-plus years of clinical experience and research. It is general in nature and not intended to be a substitute for evaluation or treatment by a competent mental health professional. If you believe you need mental health interventions, please see a specialist as soon as possible.

CONTENTS

PREFACE

INTRODUCTION TO THE SERVING IN HOSTILE PLACES SERIES

"And... we know the time, that it is already the hour for us to awake from sleep, for our salvation is now nearer than when we became believers.... The night has advanced toward dawn; the day is near. So then we must lay aside the works of darkness, and put on the weapons of light. Let us live decently as in the daytime... and make no provision for the flesh to arouse its desires."

— ROMANS 13:11-13A, 14B (NET)

I was tasked to write this series of books to help prepare men and women for Kingdom work in hostile places. Every place, of course, is hostile for true believers who live and work in our fallen world, and I don't want to minimize the stress that any follower of God feels when he or she does battle with our enemy. Strongholds, however, do exist. There are regions that are historically (and currently) more dangerous, stressful, under-reached, and volatile - where the spiritual and physical battle is more intense, and where casualties are more likely to happen. I write these books for those who want to serve in these hostile places.

This intense battle is happening in plain sight, and more people are coming, as Paul says, to "know the time" and leave their lives of comfort and safety to help usher in the new "day." The call for the church to "awake from sleep" and prepare for the coming of that day sounds with ever intense clarity as the political and moral foundations of the world collapse. Darkness is breathing its last gasp, and as the night advances toward dawn, many are choosing to "lay aside the works of darkness, put on the weapons of light" and join in the battle.

Two things become obvious when one joins this battle, however. First, this battle is not without cost. It produces real physical, emotional and spiritual casualties, and those who want to engage in the battle must be aware of these and cogently count the cost prior to enjoining it. Casualties are a normal part of battle and Christian servants are not immune to the stress that accompanies the spiritual battles they engage in. This is particularly true in those places that are very difficult to serve in, places where emotional casualties are sure to arise. As was drilled into my head during my residency training as a psychologist in the US Air Force, "Everyone who serves in the crucible of combat will become a combat fatigue victim; it's just a matter of time." In fact, the average soldier will develop stress disorders and combat fatigue after only 80 to 90 combat days.[1] Christians serving in hostile places also encounter intense stress and are prone to developing stress-related reactions over the course of their service.

Like soldiers entering combat, many Christian workers begin their service feeling invincible. It does not take long, though, until they have an experience where they face their own mortality and count the cost of their service in new and deeper ways. For many Christian international workers, their first encounter with their own mortality often occurs vicariously - when they see one of their fellow workers succumb to stress and fall in some horrific way. Alcoholism, affairs, depression, anxiety, suicide, addictions and psychotic episodes are more common among overseas Christian workers than their supporters back home can know or imagine. The goal of this book series is to provide for Kingdom workers serving in hostile places what combat psychiatry provides for soldiers, namely to prevent their break-down in combat and to facilitate their recovery when they do succumb to stress. Combat psychiatry teaches us that with proper preparation, many stress casualties can be avoided; it also teaches that with proper care, many stress related casualties can successfully return to service. **International Christian workers need combat psychiatry.**

The second thing that becomes obvious when we serve the King in hostile places is that the battle we fight is internal, spiritual, and against our own flesh more than against any external force. Paul makes this clear in Romans 13 when he talks about the concepts of flesh, darkness and living decently. Putting on the weapons of light requires that we "lay aside the works of darkness" and "make no provisions for the flesh".

For many of us, however, concepts like "darkness" and "flesh" remain abstract entities that we don't understand, let alone know how to "lay aside" or "make no provision for". When we serve the King in hostile places, however, these concepts become vitally important as we discover that much of what we really battle is our own flesh. It is our flesh, empowered by stress, that kills and destroys us; it is in laying aside our flesh that we can best deal with stress; and it is in laying aside our flesh that we can pick up the "weapons of light" and fight. **Servants of the King in hostile places need a workable model of flesh, spirit and the battle between the two.** Only when we view our effectiveness and resiliency in terms of laying aside the works of darkness and putting on the weapons of light can we truly be prepared to face the ensuing battle.

This book series walks international workers through the process of developing Godly resilience, which comes as we "live decently in the daytime...and make no provisions for the flesh...." It addresses the whole gamut of serving in hostile places, from understanding stress, to providing specific recommendations for those who train and support international workers. When finished reading this series, international workers will have a workable model of how to understand and deal with the stress of service and the ministry-killing fleshly vulnerabilities that this stress empowers.

Book one starts the series by tackling stress. Serving in hostile places is intensely stressful, and international workers and their support network must grasp exactly what stress is, and how it can damage both body and soul. Only by understanding the intensity of the stress they will face can international workers and their supporters begin to appreciate the need to deal with the flesh that this stress empowers. Although book one is written as preparation for people going to serve in hostile contexts, seasoned international workers, member care providers, family members of international workers, and church missions coordinators will all find its content insightful and provocative.

Book two addresses the unique training and support needs that international workers serving in hostile places have. They need screening, training and support that go beyond what most sending organizations provide their workers. The training and support they need is more like what special forces in the military receive. In book two, readers will find specific recommendations for psychologically screening workers, how to set up support programs that provide "unequivocal" support, and how to document and address areas of weakness without undermining the international worker's morale.

Book three focuses on developing Godly resilience. Godly resilience comes when God's love and grace are experienced in heart-changing ways in the midst of the profound stress and weakness inherent to overseas service. The program presented in book three is born from my own clinical, military and overseas experience. These are integrated with the latest advances in the neurosciences, the philosophy of the soul, and theology to help international workers resiliently rely on the spiritual power that their relationship with God gives to overcome stress and flesh.

So why am *I* writing this book series? The battle to write or not was finally determined by many people reminding me that my training, background and experiences are God-given and unique, and that He would be glorified if I write something based on the experiences and training He has given me. As I look back on my life, I can see how God has equipped me to write about this subject matter both professionally and experientially.

Professionally, He has given me over 30 years of clinical experience working in a variety of settings and with clients from multiple nationalities and ethnicities. He has also given me experience working as a psychologist in the US Air Force where I was trained and equipped to help individuals prepare for and overcome combat stress and fatigue. Since my Air Force days, much of my clinical attention and practice has focused on treating individuals who have gone through traumatic experiences. Part of my training and experience working with trauma includes over 20 years using EMDR. [2]

Experientially, I have spent the last 22 years practicing overseas, working with Christians and non-Christians from many diverse cultures and backgrounds. These experiences have been invaluable as they have provided me the opportunity to see a side of life that few others are privileged enough to see. Daily listening as others openly and honestly describe their struggles is like looking at the skeletons in people's closets, or their dirty laundry that they work hard to hide from others. Dirty laundry and skeletons help people appreciate the difficulties and struggles everyone has as he or she lives in this fallen world. It also gives a deeper understanding of just how great God's grace is.

In this book series, I will present ideas that are markedly different than those typically employed in the field of member care and will discuss why the "old ways" may not be adequate for members serving in very stressful places. My comments are not intended as criticism, but rather are humbly posited as additions to the things that others are already doing.

As you read these books I hope and expect that the theme that shines through my clinical work is visible. Specifically, I love to tell about the wonders of God's grace and love and believe that a deeper understanding of His grace and love are what are needed for us to effectively put aside our flesh and take up the weapons of light. As Paul writes to Titus, it is God's grace that "trains us to reject godless ways and worldly desires and to live self-controlled, upright, and godly lives in the present age... ".[3] The goal of this book series is to systematically lay out how God's grace trains us, and how His love transforms us.

I will adopt many abbreviations for convenience in writing. "Mission-ary" is an outdated and often dangerous term that has recently been replaced with more ambiguous and benign terms like International Worker, Overseas Worker, Christian Worker, etc.... I will also adopt the term International Worker and abbreviate it as IW (or IWs for plural) to refer to missionaries who are serving or preparing to serve long-term in a cross-cultural setting.

IWs are usually not independent, but rather belong to an agency that sends and supports them as they serve in foreign countries. These organizations might be denominationally related, interdenominational missionary organizations, or even companies that adopt a BAM (Business as Missions) model. I will lump all such missionary sending and support organizations under the heading of Sending Organizations (SOs).

Many SOs provide their IWs with support and care once they are deployed to an overseas assignment. These support services have in recent years been generally merged under the moniker of Member Care. Each SO has its own model and plan for providing these services, with some having a designated member care department, some hiring outside member care consultants or companies, and some including the support services they provide under their personnel department's responsibilities. I will refer to any person who provides member care to an IW, whether or not they are from the IW's SO, as a Member Care Provider (MCP).

How we describe the countries where IWs work is also important. Some countries are more stressful and difficult to work in and will, therefore, lead to more stress related spiritual and emotional casualties. Many, but not all, of these countries are places that are overtly hostile to Christianity and Christians and where Christians are actively persecuted for their faith. The term "hostile" captures much of the climate of these countries, and the opposite of hostile, "open" or "accepting" is a good contrasting descriptor. However, hostile does not completely capture all the stress related to serving in these places, so I will in general refer to these types of countries as not only hostile, but hazardous and perilous places as well. My fear, however, in describing these countries in this way is that I will somehow make people who serve in other countries feel belittled, criticized, or that their service is somehow not as important or respected because it is "easier". What do you call a place of service that is not "hazardous", for example? Safe or easy? I know that no such "easy" place of service exists, and I would never want to call any place where someone invests his or her life of service, and the stress they experience there, "easy".

To find a term that captures the uniqueness of a hostile or hazardous place to serve (hopefully without denigrating the stress experienced in other places of service) I have decided to adopt a term from pistol ammunition. As I hunt and hike in the backwoods of Wyoming, where there is a real possibility of encountering a mountain lion, wolf, coyote or bear, I carry a pistol with me. Normally, the ammunition my pistol shoots will be lethal to most animals I would need to defend myself against. In our model, ammunition can be representative of service in any part of the world - it is sufficiently difficult as to be lethal! My pistol can, however, also safely shoot +P rated ammunition. +P means that the bullet holds a little more powder which makes it more potent because it flies faster and hits harder. Hostile or difficult countries can be thought of as +P countries, countries where there is a more powder added to the already lethal stress load which accompanies service in any overseas assignment. Therefore, I will refer to hostile or hazardous countries as +P countries.

I wish to thank the many people who have inspired and supported me as I write. Chief among these are all the clients I have worked with over the last 30 plus years. I respect each of my clients and have learned so much from them as I've had the pleasure of walking with them through hard times. I would never want one of my former clients to read something I have written and feel belittled or singled out. Because of this, all case examples I use in these books will not refer to a real client; rather, they will be taken as conglomerates of many clients that I have seen. All identifying information will also be fictitious and is not intended to refer to any specific person.

Lisa, my wife, also deserves thanks for her support and patience. It always amazes me how she can listen to me drone on and on about some obscure topic without her eyes glazing over. My parents have also been very encouraging to me and have taught me what love really means.

I also wish to thank a beautiful country in North Africa (which shall remain unnamed) for providing me with a meaningful (though not always peaceful) place to put pen to paper or fingers to keyboard. I also wish to thank my organization, which gave me the idea to write this work and supported me throughout its writing.

Rebecca Jones has also proven invaluable. Her suggestions and editing have greatly improved the readability of this manuscript.

I place this project in God's hands as an offering of praise. I rejoice that His grace is sufficient for even me, and that He can use flawed people such as myself for His Kingdom work. My deepest hope and prayer is that you will somehow be blessed by Him as you read.

❧ I ❧

MEMBER CARE IN +P SETTINGS

...war imposes a unique kind of stress on its participants. Any normal fear of failure or disgrace in civilian life is immeasurably increased by the omnipresent danger of being killed, wounded or facing capture.[1]

-D. O'Brian

This is the section where we finally begin to discuss what can be done to prepare and support IWs who are serving the King in +P countries. I will first present recommendations for SO leadership as they consider how to set up or revise support programs for IWs in +P countries. Screening and training will be given special consideration since their proper implementation is a crucial foundation for establishing the unique care system that is most useful in hazardous settings. To illustrate how each concept and tool I recommend can be applied, I will also present an illustrative case. Finally, I will end this section with a primer on stress management. This primer will lay the foundation for the next volume of this series which will present a soul-based model for stress management and resiliency training.

As we think about supporting IWs in +P places, the recommendations I make should be understood as being specifically related to helping with emotional and spiritual support. The system I propose should not be understood as a SO's complete member care program, rather an integral part of a larger system of care. A complete member care system should also provide things not directly included in this model including medical benefits, professional development, financial support, in-country leadership, security briefings, support finding housing, etc.... These ancillary services are extremely important for IWs, and many SOs do an excellent job providing these. What I am presenting in this book series, however, is a model for helping IWs deal with the emotional stress involved in assignments in +P countries, which is often underestimated, not adequately prepared for, and handled in less than ideal ways. The program I am offering is intended to help mediate the +P stress that empowers flesh and results in IWs leaving the field prematurely.

Goals for a Member Care Program

The stress that soldiers experience in combat doesn't just come from the horrors of seeing others killed or being tasked with the unthinkable prospect of killing fellow human beings. Many argue, rather, that the most difficult thing that soldiers face in combat situations is fear of failure. Many soldiers somehow find the inner strength to deal with the actual physical trauma of combat. Those that struggle the most, who are most likely to become long-term combat stress casualties, are those who attribute the suffering of self or others to their own weaknesses and failures. "I'm the reason my friend was killed - why didn't I see that IED!", and "If only I were stronger, I wouldn't be experiencing these reactions," are common ruminations of traumatized veterans.

This tendency toward self-blame and self-loathing is a natural by-product of being in situations where danger to self and others is a realistic threat. These dangers increase the weight of daily decisions and normal fears of failure become drastically amplified. In fact, most of the interventions that military mental health professionals use to treat acute combat stress reactions are geared to help the soldier understand that their stress responses, no matter how severe they are, are normal reactions to the very dangerous situations they are exposed to. The primary goal is to help them avoid blaming their own personal weakness for their struggles or the outcome of their service. Those who are overcome with self-loathing and guilt have the worst prognosis and often struggle with chronic mental health issues. Those who can mitigate the sense of failure are more likely to recover from the stress of their service and resume their combat roles.

Because IWs serving in +P contexts also live in perilous situations, they, too, struggle with amplified fear of failure and shame about their weaknesses. The real threat of harm to self, others, and those who convert to the faith intensifies the outcome of actions and can lead to feelings of failure that are more intense than in normal situations. When these fears are not adequately dealt with, they can cause the IW to crumble and break, often becoming a ministry casualty. SO's and MCP's actions, as they attempt to lead and support the IWs they work with, can either mediate the IW's fear response, or solidify it into a chronic sense of failure. My experience is that the systems and protocols that SOs have set in place to support IWs in non +P contexts often inadvertently lead to a heightened sense of failure for IWs serving in intensely stressful +P environments.

Just recently, for example, I heard about an IW who had to be evacuated from a remote setting due to a serious illness. The IW's teammates and supervisors worked their hardest to get this IW the medical care that she needed and to evacuate her to a place with modern medical treatment. However, the IW sank into a coma and died a day after arriving at a modern hospital. It is easy to imagine the guilt and sense of failure that this IW's teammates and leaders must feel. They are likely plagued with guilt for not responding to the illness quickly enough, not discerning the severity of the situation before it was too late, not having done adequate preparations for these types of emergencies, not having enough First-Aid training to stabilize her, and for myriad other ways that their actions fell short in saving this woman's life. Fear of failing is common for most people, but this fear is greatly amplified when failure can mean the death of self or others. SOs and MCPs are in a unique position to either mitigate fear of failing, or to contribute to it and strengthen its strangle hold on the IW.

As we consider the unique needs of supporting IWs in +P contexts, I would suggest that **one of the primary goals for a SO is to create an environment where the IW is empowered to serve without fear.** When an IW serves without fear, they are more confident, effective and able to display to the world the peace that faith in the grace our Heavenly Father lavishes on us produces. They are also more resilient in the face of the intense stress they encounter, able to ride the storms of +P service without sinking under the waves of fear.

Programs that attempt to create a confident and fearless IW will find emphasizing three things helpful. We will examine each of these things in more detail in the following sections, but I will briefly outline them here.

First, a fundamental goal of a +P support program should be for MCPs **to be able to unequivocally support the people assigned to their care.** To avoid unwittingly contributing to an IW's fear of failure, and to create an atmosphere of trust where the IW can freely discuss with their MCP any issue they are struggling with (the struggles that make them fear failure), the MCP's role must be viewed as completely supportive and not growth-oriented or evaluative. Unequivocal support means that the MCP's role should not be mixed with an evaluative or growth component; their sole responsibility should be to complete support the IW as they do a very difficult job. **SOs need a milieu where IWs serving in +P contexts are viewed as psychologically healthy, spiritually mature, and professionally competent.** When people with these qualities struggle, it is not because of a weakness or lack of motivation. They struggle because they are doing an extremely difficult job in a hostile place. Since this is the case, the MCP's goal is to support them, not correct, challenge, rebuke, or improve them.

Providing unequivocal support is a challenging goal, however. To implement it often requires SOs to rethink how they typically screen and train their IWs. The benefits of unequivocal support, though, far outweigh the initial outlay of screening and training resources as IW longevity, productivity, spiritual growth and emotional stability should all increase. In the next section, I'll extensively describe how to create a milieu like this.

The second overarching goal of providing care and support to IWs serving in +P countries is to **create a bond of trust between the MCP and the IW.** IWs need to view their MCP as a safe person to discuss their struggles, fears, and tears with. The sense of safety should allow the IW to be willing to discuss all of their deepest struggles with their MCP. The goal is to prevent IWs from dealing with their struggles privately, out of reach of the SOs support services. To accomplish this, however, IWs need to feel that their struggles won't be used against them - that if they confess some failing, fear or weakness to their MCP, it won't be entered into their personnel records and somehow hinder their future service and career goals. IWs have invested so much into their move overseas that they won't risk talking with someone they fear will hinder or hurt them and their work. Their biggest fear is to be sent home as a ministry failure. As just discussed, SOs need to create a milieu where struggles are viewed as stress reactions and not as personal failures. When this milieu is in place, it makes it easier for the SO to give some limited confidentiality in the interaction between the MCP and the IW - facilitating the type of trust needed for IWs to talk about struggles they are having and receive the support they desperately need.

And finally, the third overarching goal of a SO's support program for IWs serving in +P areas involves **creating an environment of trust between the MCP and the SO**. SOs need to trust that IWs and MCPs are dealing with issues to prevent the Kingdom, ministry, and SO being damaged by some "hidden," sinful behavior. SOs need to know that sins are being addressed, that standards are being adhered to, and that IWs are not struggling in a way that will destroy their work, bring shame on our Heavenly Father, and discredit the SO. Trust between the MCP and SO can be created by procedural changes, but the appropriate screening and training of the IW is also an important foundation.

Ability to Unequivocally Support and Care for IWs

IWs who serve in +P settings need unequivocal support from their MCP and SO. A central assumption to providing **unequivocal support is the belief that IWs' struggles do not originate from any pre-existing condition or performance deficit that needs correction or treatment.** Support can, therefore, be offered without any evaluative or self-improvement motivations; the MCP can offer purely supportive and stress-mediating assistance.

In this model, the term pre-existing condition includes psychological disorders, unprocessed traumatic experiences, personality traits or disorders, and medical conditions. If these factors exist, providing categorical support is difficult since the cause of the IW's struggles are not solely attributable to stress. Unequivocal support necessitates that the SO and the MCP can say that the struggles IWs develop occur only because of stress. They happen in healthy, well-trained and equipped individuals who are overwhelmed by the stress of the job they are doing - not because of other factors. Unfortunately, many MCPs and SOs cannot approach IW struggles with this attitude. This happens because the screening and training programs of many SOs are not designed to ensure that other causes (i.e., pre-existing conditions) of IW struggles are ruled out.

To illustrate this distinction, let's look at a soldier who has an intense reaction while serving in combat. This soldier is hallucinating, unresponsive to questions, and unable to sleep or eat. The best outcome for both the soldier and the war effort is for the people who are tasked with helping this soldier to be able to say, "This is a normal soldier who is having an intense stress reaction related to serving in combat. His symptoms are not related to anything other than combat stress." When the care provider is able to say this, then the soldier can be given rest, his symptoms normalized (i.e., he can be explicitly told this is a normal stress reaction), and he can receive healing support from his care provider, support that is solely designed to rectify his stress related issues and not to cure or treat other problems that might be causing his symptoms. Research that I studied during my training as an Air Force psychologist showed that the vast majority of soldiers whose combat stress responses are treated in this way can return to combat duty after three days of rest.

However, if there are questions about what the symptoms the soldier is experiencing really mean (e.g., Is this soldier's symptoms signs of a schizophrenia and not just a normal stress reaction?), then the care provider will not be able to provide the nonjudgmental support that the soldier most needs. Rather, the care provider's support will be hindered by the need to assess what the true cause of the soldier's reactions are. This assessment will lead to decisions about the soldier's suitability to continue service. The military helps care providers determine that the emotional struggles soldiers have are stress related (and only stress related) by employing screening measures and training that weed out individuals with pre-existing conditions, conditions that will make understanding the cause of future stress responses difficult to determine.

SOs can learn from the military. If a SO's screening and training programs do not adequately weed out individuals with pre-existing conditions, it will make it very difficult for their MCPs to provide unequivocal support to their IWs. Rather the MCP will be bogged down with trying to answer the question: "Is this a normal stress reaction, or does it represent a pre-existing issue that makes this IW unqualified for future service?". Proper screening and training protocols will help MCPs be able to say with confidence that what the IW is dealing with is purely the stress reaction of a normal person serving in a very difficult place and not indicative of a pre-existing psychological condition. Only when the MCP can, with confidence, say that the IW is a normal person having stress reactions can they provided the much needed and effective nonjudgmental support.

SOs, MCPs and IWs all need to view IWs serving in +P countries as the Navy SEALS of the IW community. Navy SEALS are the cream of the American military, and the trident badge they proudly wear after they have undergone their intense training and screening program proves their physical, tactical and emotional excellence. When a Navy

SEAL enters combat and has a stress reaction or develops PTSD, no one would attribute their struggles to some deficit in their skills, training, motivation or maturity. Likewise, if a Navy SEAL is injured in combat, the whole care system is designed for their help and recovery. No one looks for ways to improve the SEAL, to correct him, or to mentor him to better heights of service. They just provide support - unequivocally. IWs who serve in +P countries need to be viewed as navy SEALs: They are the cream of the IW community who have been screened, trained and certified. Support given to them in time of need is given without question or fear that something else is needed.

Let me illustrate with a case example. Imagine with me an IW who begins seeing demons looking in the windows of his house soon after arriving in his country of service. The resulting panic and fear that this causes makes the IW clingy and needy on his teammates, demanding that they meet at his house to pray for hours each evening to fend off the satanic attack. If the teammates don't come and pray with him for the necessary length of time, this young IW feels too afraid to sleep and is unable to perform his language study and work assignment the next day. Sleeplessness, and seeing demons taunting him each night in his windows, contribute to the IW's stress level, poor work performance, and increasingly depressed mood.

Is this a stress reaction of a normal IW serving in a very difficult place? The SO's screening and training procedures should be designed to ensure that this is the case. If the SO has properly evaluated this IW (so that psychological conditions such as Posttraumatic Stress Disorder, Bipolar Affective Disorder, Histrionic Personality Disorder, Schizophrenia, etc...; and medical conditions such as neurological problems or seizure disorder can all be ruled out), then the MCP can provide this IW with unequivocal support. Unequivocal support in this situation would include the MCP being armed with compassion and empathy as he or she works to support the IW. Interventions could then include understanding, listening, prayer and counsel for dealing with stress and spiritual warfare. The MCP could also help the IW's team members understand that this is a spiritual and stress related reaction and that their teammate is a normal individual engaging in battle, who needs support.

If, however, the SO has not provided adequate screening and training, then the MCP will not be able to provide nonevaluative support to the IW. Rather, he or she will have to try to answer the question, "What do these experiences mean?" Having to answer this question will change the relationship that the IW and MCP have. The MCP will have to determine if the IW is suitable for overseas work, and the IW will view the MCP as someone who is there to evaluate him or her and not just provide the support that is needed. I believe, therefore, that it is imperative for SOs to properly screen and train their IWs who serve in +P countries. **To provide IWs with the unequivocal support they need, all parties need to have some level of confidence that any struggles the IW develops are exclusively due to stress reactions.**

Before we begin looking at specific recommendations for screening and training IWs, we need to first briefly address a common fear that MCPs and SOs have - the fear that providing unequivocal support will harm IWs. This fear represents the same dilemma that is faced by people who work with the poor and indigent - the fear that providing support will make the person dependent, weak, less trusting in God, or enable a destructive behavioral pattern. I have personally wrestled with how to best help the beggars I frequently see on the streets of the developing countries I've served in. Will the money they are asking for really help them? Or, will it be turned over to the pimp who is forcing them to beg, used to feed an addiction, or enable a lazy person to avoid the real-life demands of working? As Steve Corbett and Brian Fikkert remind us in their well-received book, *When Helping Hurts*,[2] even with the best of intentions, providing help to someone in need can actually be harmful if done improperly.

Consciously or unconsciously, MCPs can approach support work with the conviction that more than support is needed. In this model, the MCP perceives the IW's struggles as coming from someplace other than the stress of doing their difficult jobs; struggles represent a weakness that needs to be corrected. The MCP's goal becomes one of correcting, exhorting, building up, evaluating and mentoring so as to prevent the IW from being complacent in their struggles and not growing. To return to our beggar analogy, an IW who is struggling is analogous to a beggar who is seen as living on the street because they are lazy, weak, mentally ill, not motivated, or lacking skills or training. Care for these people often looks like mentoring, correcting, training and even rebuking - not supporting them. If an IW's struggles are viewed as arising from weaknesses like these, then the MCP runs the risk of harming the IW by his or her interventions, destroying self-esteem and motivation in the process of caring. These types of interventions fuel the IW's fear of failure that was discussed earlier.

The model of care that I'm advocating is one where the struggling IW is viewed as a combat casualty. They have struggles and fall not because of personal weakness, lack of training, or psychological problems, but because they are fighting a war and have an enemy that is bent on their destruction. Unequivocal support (and member care), therefore, is analogous to a military medic running into the heat of battle to pick up, treat and comfort an injured comrade; there is no evaluation, no questioning of ability or motivation, no desire to improve the casualty's performance - only the provision of care and treatment.

The model of support I'm advocating is NOT like a well-meaning wealthy person handing a beggar a fistful of dollars. SOs are right to be concerned that inappropriate ways of supporting their IWs can lead to dependence, lack of growth, and further escalation of problems. Rather, the type of support I'm suggesting is more analogous to a wealthy benefactor giving money to a person that is healthy, normal, motivated, spiritually mature - but who temporarily needs some financial assistance to better do his or her job. There is no fear in giving this type of support.

In the next section, I present recommendations that will help SOs create the type of atmosphere where providing this type of nonjudgmental support is possible. How the person is screened and trained is a very important part of this process.

Screening

There is no such thing as a perfect IW. All IWs will bring emotional, physical and spiritual vulnerabilities with them to their overseas service. In fact, my experience suggests that God leaves at least one area of struggle or weakness in each person's life that they are not able to overcome by their own efforts; IWs are no exception. This area of weakness keeps people from being self-righteous and shows them the wonders of God's all-sufficient grace. I think there is a scriptural basis to argue that as people are used more by God and get closer to Him, their areas of weakness and struggle will become even more pronounced[3] and insurmountable.

This suggests that no matter how thorough a SO's screening methods, all IWs will bring "baggage" (emotional and spiritual weaknesses or vulnerabilities) with them as they serve overseas. Not all baggage, however, is the same, and a SO's mandate in screening and preparing the IWs for +P service is to ensure that they screen out individuals who have excess "check-in baggage", only allowing those with "carry-on bags" to serve in high stress areas.

"Carry-on baggage" is what God designed IWs to travel with as it keeps them humble and dependent on His grace. Carry-on baggage can be thought of as Paul's thorn in the flesh - something that God used to keep him humble and not puffed-up with pride. Indeed, when Jesus sends out the twelve, he exhorts them to not carry any baggage with them,[4] but only what was in hand.

"Check-in baggage", however, slows the IW and SO down, is a burden that the whole team must deal with, becomes a spiritual and emotional vulnerability that the devil uses to attack, and forces the MCP to deal with it rather than provide unequivocal support. Check-in baggage is problematic, stressful to deal with, and often incurs additional expenses as the interventions that SOs must use to take care of it are costly and labor intensive.

SOs might not be able to screen out all issues, but I think they can identify people with excess baggage, baggage that will grow to be an ever-increasing burden and drain on the team and SO's resources. As you can imagine, excess baggage is particularly problematic in war zones and high stress areas like +P countries. Service in +P countries needs people who are emotionally mobile and not weighed down or slowed down by too much emotional weight. When an IW brings too much baggage to a +P country of service, it quickly becomes something more than a personal issue as the whole team and SO are tasked with helping to carry the load. People carrying excess baggage need to be screened out and not sent as IWs to +P assignments.

Determining what constitutes too much baggage is not easy, however. SO leadership often want to set the baggage weight limit at a high level; field leadership and MCPs argue for a very low limit. SOs balk at screening out too much baggage because they are under pressure to find and send workers into the harvest. SO leadership know how rare qualified and healthy applicants are, and often argue that an applicant's excess baggage won't cause that much problem. SO leadership hopes that baggage will go away once the IW is allowed to pursue their dreams and serve God overseas. Some even argue that people with excess baggage often benefit from the supportive environment and discipleship opportunities that overseas service and team life provide, allowing them to become viable, long-term IWs.

MCPs and field leadership want high standards and low baggage weight limits, however, since they have seen the damage that someone carrying excess baggage can do to team and ministry. MCP and field leadership have often picked up the pieces caused when someone's baggage becomes a team and ministry destroying problem. They have seen well-qualified IWs jump ship when one of their teammate's baggage is too heavy to bear and starts to rock the whole boat. Team problems are, after all, the number one reason why IWs leave the field early, and team problems often have excess baggage as their root cause.

A balance must exist, however. In order to provide unequivocal support to their IWs serving in +P countries, SOs need to ensure that their IWs are carrying the right amount of baggage. The goal, however, is not IW perfection. **The goal is to be able to certify that the IW is free of excess vulnerabilities and not carrying pre-existing problems which will prevent the SOs MCP from providing them with the unequivocal support that they need.** The goal of screening and training should be to assure the SO, MCPs, and all team members that problems that arise during service represent only stress reactions and not a personality disorder or other form of psychopathology. If this goal can be achieved, then it will have a hugely positive impact on team relationships and the type and quality of care the MCPs can provide. Proper screening will allow teams to support each other as normal people doing a very difficult job; they won't have to wonder if the struggles a teammate is going through represents excess baggage that they shouldn't have been allowed to bring and that will sink the whole team boat. No IW should ever have to say, "It's not fair that my teammate brought all this excess baggage out here that we all have carry for them now." Proper screening will allow the MCP to not be involved in making evaluative decisions about the IW, but to be able to unconditionally stand behind the IW and provide unequivocal support.

Let me provide an example of an IW with excess baggage, and how the excess baggage grew into team problems requiring the MCP to become involved in decision making rather than providing support. Jan (a confabulated case based on multiple similar situations) comes from a dysfunctional family in the US. As a child, Jan's father was strict and angry with her, frequently belittling her, pointing out how she disappointed him, and never providing her with any affirmation. He told her on many occasions that he wished she had never been born because she was such a worthless person. Her mother was powerless in the face of her father's anger and suspicions, and the two of them frequently argued and occasionally resorted to physical violence. When things would get really bad at home, Jan would escape by spending the night with her best friend. On one such occasion, her friend's father sexually molested Jan. She barely escaped being raped, but her friend's father threatened to kill her and her whole family if she ever told anyone about what happened. Scarred and depressed, Jan turned to her faith for comfort. Though the dysfunction at home worsened, she grew in her faith.

Her faith journey, however, was not without trials. When she first started dating at age 15, her 19-year-old boyfriend pushed the physical limits of their relationship too far for her comfort. The memories of her prior sexual assault came flooding back and induced a depressive episode. During this time, her faith dried up, God felt far away, and she was overwhelmed with feelings of worthlessness.

To relieve her emotional pain, Jan turned to cutting the inside of her thighs with a razor. On two occasions she overdosed on over-the-counter medications, hoping that it would be enough to end her existence, which it was not. She never told anyone about the cutting or the suicide attempts, and after a very terrible year-and-a-half, Jan was again renewed by her faith and relationship with God. She managed to graduate high school and enter college as a nutrition major. It was during this time in her life that she felt led into missions and began applying to be an IW. On her application with her SO, she noted one of her motivations to be and IW was to grow and find a supportive environment where she could work through the pains that her family and early experiences had caused. Later, she told her MCP that her team was the first experience she had of a loving and accepting family.

Once on the field, Jan became overwhelmed by the stress of living in a foreign country and working closely with equally stressed teammates. She bonded well with one family on her team, however, and spent as much time with them as possible. Her relationships with her single teammates was, however, stormy: She loved some and felt intimidated by and feared others. She was extremely sensitive to any perceived slights and would have panic attacks in the evenings if she felt even a hint of criticism or correction. She described any correction or dissatisfaction as feeling like her father's emotional abuse, which would send her into an emotional tailspin for hours or days. When distressed, she would cling to the family that she felt attached to and supported by.

At first the family was glad to support and help Jan through her emotional struggles. However, as her distress level went up, her demands became more and more frequent and intense, and she would try to spend every available minute she could basking in this family's supportive care. She also really enjoyed the affirmation that the father of this family gave to her and began to idealize him. She described the wife as being friendly, but distant, and whenever she went to visit this family would gravitate towards talking with the husband. Although neither Jan nor the husband had any bad intentions, Jan's constant neediness and dependence on him began to make his wife jealous. "All you ever do is try to help Jan," she complained to her husband. "You don't have any time or energy left over for me or the kids. Maybe you are attracted to this pretty young woman and want to be with her more than me."

The couple agreed that they needed to set limits on Jan and started telling her that they were busy in the evenings. Jan immediately understood this meant they didn't want her coming over and felt very hurt. The anxiety attack she had the first time they told her not to come lasted several hours and was only able to be calmed when she texted the husband and got his assurance that they hadn't rejected or abandoned her. To calm her, he invited her back to their house for a movie with the kids the following evening. This pattern continued for a month, with Jan's anxiety becoming more frequent and intense whenever she was not allowed to visit the family.

The family became overwhelmed by what they perceived as Jan's manipulations and decided it was time to set firm limits on her; they told her that she could only come over during team meetings from now on. Jan took this as rejection and abandonment and angrily asked how they could leave her alone to deal with all these negative emotions in the middle of this godforsaken country. "Don't you know how helpful it is to me to be around a functional family for once?" She asked? "If I don't have your support, I don't know how I'll be able to handle my life and work here!"

Jan soon sank into an angry and bitter depression. She withdrew from the family and began neglecting her work assignment. She felt distant from God and that He also must really despise her. When the MCP came to visit the team a few weeks later, Jan complained how everyone had rejected her and wasn't helping her deal with the emotional trauma she was going through. "How can they be so heartless? If only they would be kind to me, I could make it here", she said. She also confessed to her MCP that she had had one episode where she was so overwhelmed by her feelings of rejection that she had kicked the brick wall in her apartment until her foot was so sore and bruised that she had troubles walking on it for a week. She was also having urges to cut herself again, but had, so far, been able to avoid them. The hopelessness and suicidal thoughts of her past depressive episode felt like they were just around the corner, waiting to come back.

Jan's team was overwhelmed by her neediness and divisiveness. They viewed her as manipulative, self-focused and extremely volatile. Her tantrums and "panic attacks" became team issues that required hours of supportive assistance. They were all frustrated to the point that they said something had to be done about Jan or they wouldn't be able to survive any longer. The MCP, although she wanted to help and provide Jan with the support she needed, knew that if Jan continued serving as she was, that the team would fall apart and that the SO would lose at least half of the well-qualified and productive IWs on the team. She finally recommended that Jan needed to return to the US for treatment and evaluation of her depression, neediness, panic attacks and emotional volatility. Her interventions were too late, however, for Jan's teammates. Two of them left the field a few months after Jan was sent home, saying that they couldn't deal with the prospect of having another teammate like Jan in the future.

Three Core Screening Areas

Any candidate who wants to serve in a +P setting should undergo a screening that emphasizes the assessment of three core areas. **The first core emphasis of assessment should be to rule out personality disorders or strong personality traits.** Personality disorders are marked by rigid ways of thinking and behaving that detrimentally effect a person's ability to control their emotions and lead to relationship problems[5]. There are 10 personality disorders commonly described in psychological literature, but my experience has shown that two of them, Borderline and Narcissistic personality disorders, are the ones that most commonly wreak havoc on IW team relationships and ministry. Jan, in our previous example, likely had Borderline Personality Disorder or strong borderline personality traits. Although some non +P places of service might have enough ancillary and team support systems set in place to allow someone with strong personality traits or a personality disorder to successfully serve there, +P countries will lack the level of support needed and are not appropriate. The stress and lack of support in +P countries will make team and ministry even more vulnerable to the damage that a teammate with a personality disorder can do. I, therefore, recommend that a SO's assessment protocol should include some method to assess for, and rule-out, personality disorders or strong traits.

Second, screening should also focus on ruling out fleshly vulnerabilities which may be empowered by the intense stress of serving in +P countries. These vulnerabilities can include such things as addictions and a history of impulsive, self-injurious or suicidal behaviors. My experience has been that, even if a candidate has had many years of freedom from these types of behaviors while living in their home country, these vulnerabilities can take on new life when fueled by the stress of serving in +P countries, rearing their ugly head in team and ministry-destroying ways. An IW who developed alcohol dependence while serving in a +P country is an example. This man hadn't had any alcohol related problems since he was in college and had served in a non +P country for several years with no problems. However, when he moved to a +P country, the intense stress and spiritual battle he encountered caused a relapse and he had to resign his position in disgrace and return to his home country for rehabilitation. Because of the possibility of stress-induced relapse of addictions, I recommend that IW screening procedures also include a thorough assessment of destructive behaviors and addictions.

And finally, conditions which will put the individual at risk for developing intense anxiety reactions or destabilizing emotionally (into depression or even psychotic conditions) need to be screened for and ruled out. This is not necessarily an easy task, however. Military research, for example, has found that it is difficult to predict which soldiers will develop stress reactions when they face combat, and which won't. The best predictor that the military has identified is the presence of a diagnosable mental health condition prior to the soldier entering combat[6]. Soldiers who bring depression, anxiety, or bipolar disorder into combat are much more likely to develop conditions such as Posttraumatic Stress Disorder (PTSD) than those who don't. Other than the presence of a psychological disorder, there is little else that consistently discriminates between soldiers who will develop combat stress reactions and those that don't. This suggests that screening for the presence of mental health conditions should be a major focus of assessing a candidate's fitness for serving in the stress of a +P country.

Before we look at specific recommendations for screening of candidates, the importance of the training program that I will outline in following sections should be emphasized. The goal of the screening and training process is to allow the SO and MCP to provide the unequivocal support that the IW needs while serving in a +P country. All IWs, however, will have weaknesses and vulnerabilities that they bring to service with them. The goal of screening is to separate out those who carry excess loads of these vulnerabilities and who will likely crumble under the stress of +P service, leading to their own suffering and damage to the ministry and team. The goal of the training component is to teach IWs who have been properly screened how to deal with the normal stress reactions they will encounter in ways that will facilitate their ministry, lead to spiritual growth, and ensure healthy team functioning. What we are aiming for are IWs who have been thoroughly screened and trained to the point that the SO and MCP can certify them as "battle ready", meaning, that any issue that comes up will be because of stress, not because of excess emotional baggage or lack of training. We want people who serve in +P countries to be the "Navy SEALs" of the IW community. When a Navy SEAL struggles emotionally, no one will say that this is due to lack of motivation, training, or psychological weakness. All will say, "He or she must be under a lot of stress to struggle in this way; How can we support this hero who is doing a very difficult job?" This is the attitude that screening and training needs to foster in SOs and MCPs.

One final caveat before we begin our discussion about specific screening methods has to do with the form that the screening report should take. I, personally, have read and written many psychological screening reports for IW candidates. The typical structure of these reports includes sections that provide background information on the candidate, a summary of the psychological testing results, a description of personality traits and interpersonal styles, some speculation about what type of teammate the candidate will be, and a final section with recommendations and summary. Recommendations typically include an overall assessment of the candidate's emotional and psychological suitability to serve overseas, some assessment of the candidate's resiliency, emotional health, and interpersonal skills. Psychologist usually summarize their recommendations by giving a "Yes" recommendation, a "Yes with concerns", a "Needs further assessment", or a "Not recommended".

This type of screening process often serves IWs and SOs well when their members are heading to non +P countries. However, because of the more intense stress inherent in +P service, I suggest some revisions of the screening process and report structure for +P candidates. My opinion is that screening should focus on the three core areas identified above. Screening should, for example, focus on determining the presence of personality disorders or strong traits, the existence of fleshly vulnerabilities such as addictions, and whether or not the person has pre-existing mental health concerns, rather than on providing information about their interpersonal styles.

Because of this focus, I recommend that the psychologist involved in the screening process try to answer specific questions about the candidate rather than providing descriptors of their general functioning. For example, the psychologist's assessment should be geared to answer the question, "Does this person have a personality disorder or intense personality traits that would likely cause team relationship problems in a highly stressful environment?", rather than describing the person as having a more analytical or intuitive problem-solving style.

A decision-making rubric can then be designed based on the "yes" or "no" answers provided by psychological assessment. For example, any candidate who has a personality disorder, bipolar disorder, a history of suicide attempts, or posttraumatic stress disorder is likely not suitable to serve in +P countries. Again, the goal of the screening (and training) process is to enable the SO and MCPs to say that this person is "certified" as acceptable to serve in a high-stress environment. Once a person is certified by screening and training, the evaluation process stops and the person is unequivocally supported; they are the SEAL who is screened, trained and equipped to the utmost of the SO's ability. They are the pride and joy of the SO, and any struggle that they develop on the field can be viewed as stress related. Their struggles should not lead to the MCP or the SO's field leadership to say, "Why did we ever send this person there?"

With these goals in mind, we can now look specifically at what a screening and training program can look like.

Core 1: Mental Health Conditions

A primary focus when screening IWs for +P service should be to rule-out mental health conditions. Military psychiatry has discovered that the presence of a mental health condition is the best predictor for those who will develop combat stress reactions. Psychological screening for +P candidates should, therefore, have as one of its primary purposes to provide an answer to the question:

Does this person have a diagnosable mental health condition?

A psychologist can employ many methods to help answer this question. In addition to an interview, I personally find psychometric instruments such as the Minnesota Multiphasic Personality Inventory (MMPI) in one of its various forms, the Personality Assessment Inventory (PAI), the Beck Depression Inventory (BDI), the Beck Anxiety Inventory (BAI), a symptom checklist scale (like the Symptom Checklist-90), and the Trauma Symptoms Inventory for Adults (TSI-A) to be useful. When combined with a clinical interview and history, these psychological tests are examples of those that allow for a robust understanding of the candidates overall psychological functioning. Other psychologists, however, may prefer other testing methods to help answer this question.

The presence of a psychological condition should not instantly disqualify an individual from +P service. However, based on seeing the struggles of many IWs as they serve overseas, I recommend that some mental health conditions should be viewed as likely disqualifying for +P service. These include:

Generalized Anxiety Disorder
Bipolar Spectrum Disorders (even if successfully managed with medications)
Major Depression
Eating Disorders
Posttraumatic Stress Disorder
Psychotic Disorders
Gross Cognitive Impairments
Autism Spectrum Disorders
Adult Attention-Deficit Hyperactivity Disorder
Impulse Control Disorders

Other mental health issues should also be carefully evaluated for how they may affect the person when they enter the highly stressful +P service environment.

Mental Health Treatment History

Predicting how someone will behave in the future, especially when they are in a novel culture and situation, is extremely difficult, and psychologists will admit that we are not very good at it. A maxim that I learned in graduate school, however, has proven helpful to me in many clinical situations where I must try to predict someone's future behavior (such as risk for suicide). This maxim is: "Past behavior is the best predictor for future behavior." Because of this, assessing a person's history of mental health conditions should also be part of any screening for workers applying for +P assignments. Even though this provides historical data about conditions that might not currently be influencing the person, the information that is gleaned from this assessment will still help a trained psychologist have some insight into how a person might respond under stressful conditions.

Specific questions I like to see answered include:

Has this person ever received treatment for any mental health condition or symptom (including psychotherapy, counseling, pastoral counseling, soul care, prayer resolution ministry, inpatient or outpatient hospitalization, substance abuse treatment, etc...)?

Has this person ever taken psychotropic medications for any condition (including those prescribed by a family physician for "nerves", anxiety, grief, depression, eating disorders, or sleep problems)?

A positive history of mental health treatment should not immediately rule-out anyone from +P service; however, these conditions may give indications for how the person will respond under intense stress. A candidate with a history of treatment for more serious issues (for example, a year-long major depressive episode) should be carefully considered.

Unresolved Abuse History

Trauma is, unfortunately, something that is all too common in modern life, and many candidates will have experienced some difficult things in their history. A Trauma history does not make someone unsuitable for service in +P countries; however, significant unresolved trauma may.

When we talk about unresolved trauma, psychologists generally mean trauma that leads to dissociation in neural networks. Describing specifically what this means is beyond the scope of our discussion right now, but the basic meaning is that trauma that has not been integrated into a person's life story or personality will continue to affect their emotional regulation systems, relationships and mood in often unconscious ways.

Daniel Siegel provides a cogent summary of the effects of unresolved trauma when he says that it leads to either a person being emotionally chaotic or rigid in their responses to others or stress[7]. Being emotionally chaotic means that the individual is tossed around by many unconscious factors that lead to intense and unexpected emotional responses. Rigidity refers to having to have things in a certain way before normal emotional functioning can take place (e.g., a team member who feels unsafe unless all members of the team meet for prayer twice a day). I would also add that unresolved traumas are associated with emotional neediness, where the person feels that he or she is unable to function properly without the frequent and intense care and concern of teammates. Given these factors, it is no surprise that many of the team difficulties I have worked with throughout the years seem directly related to the effects of unresolved traumas in a team member's life.

To assess for the presence of unresolved traumas, I have found the Trauma Symptom Inventory for adults[8] to be a useful scale. Also, to better understand the amount of childhood trauma a person has experienced, the 10-question questionnaire used in the Adverse Childhood Experiences studies (conducted by the Center for Disease Control and Prevention in conjunction with Kaiser-Permanente[9]), may be helpful. (A self-test and description of the questionnaire can be found on the web page listed in this footnote.[10])

These scales, and information gleaned from clinical interview, history, and other psychological testing results, will be helpful in answering the following questions:

Does this person have a clinically significant trauma history?

Does this person have symptoms of Posttraumatic Stress Disorder (PTSD)?

Is there any indication that this person has significant unresolved trauma?

Does this person experience intense of excessive anxiety, worry, fears or phobias that do not meet the criterion for a diagnosis?

Core 2: Personality Assessment

Psychological screening for IWs heading to +P assignments should also address the second core screening area, assessing for personality disorders and strong personality traits. Screening should also provide a brief description of the individual's typical personality functioning. The specific questions that this section of the evaluation should be designed to answer are:

Does the person have a personality disorder(s) or strong personality traits (especially Borderline or Narcissistic)?

How do you expect this person's personality to be expressed in a hostile and stressful environment?

Individual psychologists will employ different tests and techniques to answer these questions. The Millon Clinical Multiaxial Inventory (MCMI), the Personality Assessment Inventory (PAI), and the Wisconsin Personality Disorders Inventory (WISPI) are typical examples and provide valuable information for psychologists as they assess for personality disorders and traits.

Some SO administrators may argue against the inclusion of so many psychological tests since they are time consuming and expensive. I can understand these concerns; but, having seen the countless hours and investment of huge financial resources to stabilize and evacuate IWs who struggle from the field, I believe that the expenditure of time and finances to do a thorough screening is well worth it. As the cost-benefit ratio for psychological testing is evaluated, the cost of the loss of one or two long-term IWs because of burn-out related to team problems should also be considered. Each individual who leaves the field because of team problems represents a huge loss to the SO, both financially and in experience. When an inappropriately screened IW decompensates or causes team problems, the damage to the ministry and Kingdom work can also be immense. Especially when considering service in +P countries, I cannot over-emphasize the necessity of screening out personality disorders and strong personality traits.

Core 3: Fleshly Vulnerabilities

The third core area of +P service screening is assessing for fleshly vulnerabilities. Since +P service is by nature extremely stressful, it will likely empower underlying fleshly weaknesses in IWs. While all IWs bring fleshly vulnerabilities with them to service, these do not lead to the same outcome. As the Apostle John says, not all sin (or fleshly weakness) is the same[11]. Some leads to death, while some does not. I believe this understanding can be applied to IWs as well. Some types of weaknesses that IWs bring to service with them will result in humility, repentance and growth as the IW discovers anew the wonder of God's grace, acceptance, and willingness to use a cracked, earthen vessel for His purposes. However, there are other types of fleshly weaknesses that, like excess emotional baggage, will overwhelm the individual IW, cause team issues, and lead to the "death" of the ministry.

The marriage relationship provides a good example of the difference between the two types of fleshly vulnerabilities. All spouses bring weakness into the marriage relationship. These require the couple to grow in mutual forgiveness, extending grace, developing patience and learning to love a less than perfect person. In his book, *Sacred Marriage*, Gary Thomas argues that God's purpose for marriage is for the couple to grow in holiness as they develop the spiritual disciplines that living so intimately with another fallen human being requires. These types of weaknesses, however, do not lead to death in the marriage (though they can if not handled appropriately). There are types of weaknesses or fleshly vulnerabilities that do kill a marriage. These include things like unfaithfulness, contempt, violence and bitterness. In the same way, the struggles that IWs bring to overseas service can bring about either growth, or death, depending on the type of weaknesses.

So, what types of fleshly vulnerabilities will likely lead to team, family, and ministry death as they are empowered by the stressors of serving in +P countries? While there are many of these, the ones that can be identified by psychological assessment, in my opinion, fall into two main categories: **1.) Self-injurious behaviors, and 2.) Impulsive or addictive behaviors.** +P candidate screening would be well-served if it includes an assessment of these two areas.

A clinical interview and the collection of historical data is often the best method to assess for the possible presence of vulnerabilities in these areas. The idea behind collecting this type of historical data is that fleshly vulnerabilities that were once turned to during times of distress or emotional upheaval easily return when the individual encounters other highly stressful situations.

I am reminded of cases of struggling IWs I have dealt with in the past. For example, years ago I worked with a young woman who had a history of cutting behaviors during a period of depression that happened several years before she began serving on the field. She had not struggled with urges to harm herself for many years until she encountered the intense interpersonal stressors of overseas service. When I met her, she was struggling with depression, anxiety and panic attacks. Even though she didn't engage in cutting behaviors, she, and her team, were all worried that her emotional distress might overwhelm her ability to resist the urge to harm herself. Fear for her safety became a means she used to manipulate her teammates into providing her with emotional support and became an intense drain on them. They feared that if they said no to her request for closeness during a time of distress, she might harm herself. She ensured everyone that she was safe as long as she could turn to them for support during her really difficult times.

Addictive behaviors and substance abuse are also issues that are prone to raise their ugly heads under intense stress. Several men I have worked with have struggled with compulsive masturbation or have resumed a pornography addiction as ways to comfort themselves during episodes of high stress. Some have also struggled with a relapse into alcohol abuse. Many times, these men report having had few or no problems in these areas for many years prior to serving in high stress situations.

Specific questions that I like to see answered by a psychological screening in this area include:

Self-Injurious Behaviors

Is there a history of significant suicidal ideation or suicide attempts?

Is there a history of cutting or other self-mutilation?

Is there a history of significant eating disorders?

Substance Abuse / Addictions:

Does this person currently drink alcohol? If so, how frequently? How much?

Does this person ever drink beverages stronger than wine or beer (e.g., Vodka, Liquor, Scotch, Gin, etc....)?

Has this person ever had alcohol related problems (i.e., drunk driving arrest, relationship problems, lost jobs, etc....)?

Has this person ever used illicit drugs (including marijuana)?

How would you describe this person's use of pornography?

- **No current or history of pornography use.**
- **History of periodic pornography use, but no current (for one year) use.**
- **History of intense or addictive pornography use, but no current (for one year) use.**
- **Periodic struggles (i.e., less than one incidence every two months).**
- **Occasional use (i.e., no more than one incidence a month).**
- **Weekly or daily use.**

Has this person ever participated in specific interventions or treatments for pornography or sex addictions?

Categorically ruling out someone based on their history is not necessarily appropriate. However, I would be very concerned sending someone with a significant history of suicide attempts, cutting, or substance abuse to a highly stressful +P assignment without ensuring appropriate support and monitoring methods.

Regarding other questionable cases (e.g., a young man who had a history of intense pornography use when he was 17, but has only "occasionally slipped" for the past five years; or another man who binge drank in college, but has not touched alcohol since) I would suggest applying a general rule-of-thumb, which I have derived solely from my clinical experience and is not necessarily scientifically based. This rule-of-thumb states that you can take a person's worst example of a given behavior in their past (e.g., daily pornography use, binge drinking, or cutting) and estimate that there is a 65% chance that he or she will return to the same level of destructive behaviors at some time during the time they live in the stress of a +P assignment. In other words, if a young man binge drank in college five years ago, we can estimate that there is a 65% chance he will struggle with binge drinking at some point in time during his tenure of service in a +P country.

A SO can use this rule-of-thumb in placement decisions by asking themselves if the 65% chance of this person struggling with binge drinking is a suitable risk to take. If they decide that placing this man is worth the risk, then I suggest their member care program needs to be carefully examined to ensure that it is set up to provide him with the support, confidentiality, and professional back-up care that he may require.

One mediating factor in this rule-of-thumb is time since the last episode of the behavior. A 45 year-old, for example, who hasn't cut herself in 30 years is much less likely to resort to cutting herself under times of stress, than a 23 year-old who hasn't cut herself in five years.

Other Useful Areas of Assessment

In addition to these three core areas that should be assessed in candidates who want to serve in +P countries, I suggest it is also helpful to screen a person's physical health, motivation, and family circumstances. Understanding these forces in an applicant's life will provide a clearer picture of possible vulnerabilities that may affect him or her during service in highly stressful +P places. An interview, or a written history form completed by the candidate, may be adequate methods to assess these variables.

Physical Conditions

Because the physical and emotional are so tightly intertwined, candidate screenings for people who want to serve in +P countries should also include an assessment of any physical conditions that may be related to emotional factors, or which might contribute to poor emotional adjustment under intense stress. Thyroid conditions, fibromyalgia, Crohn's disease, irritable bowel syndrome, seizure disorder, migraines, and many autoimmune disorders have all been shown to be exacerbated or caused by intense stress.

An individual who has a stress-related physical condition should not be automatically ruled-out for +P service. However, given that the intense stress of +P service puts the individual at increased risk for exacerbation of stress-related conditions, the SO needs to assess the impact that these conditions may have on service and physical and emotional health. Since many +P countries don't have modern medical facilities needed to treat some stress-related conditions, the availability of medical and psychological services needed to treat acute flair-ups should also be assessed.

Motivation

The motivation that drives an IW to go the field can be a big mediator in their ability to handle stress. I have seen numerous cases, for example, where an IW's family situation at home complicates their ability to get the help they need when issues develop overseas. In these situations, what I often see is that the IW was partially motivated for overseas service because it afforded an opportunity to run from a bad family situation in their home country. When they develop problems while serving overseas, it is difficult for them to return home for much needed help because there is no support or help for him or her there. I have had many IWs who are in crisis and need to be sent home for treatment tell me that sending them home would be the worst thing that could happen to them since it would only separate them from the only people who have ever really cared for them in their life - their IW team. Since they have no support from family at home, they feel that it would be much better for them to stay and work through their problems on the field with their supportive teammates. The major problem with this, however, is that these IW's emotional instability is toxic to team life.

I have also found that some individuals are motivated to serve, overseas because of economic stressors in their home country, or because they can't find a better job. While this is sometimes understandable, economic motivation is often not a good long-term prognosticator for individuals serving in highly stressful, +P, countries. The stress of service in these countries is just not worth the limited financial stability that is gained, and the individual will likely lose their motivation and prematurely quit service when the going gets rough.

Finally, I have noticed that some individuals think IW service will provide them with identity, helping them prove to themselves or others that they are a "good" Christian, or somehow help them resolve some internal conflict. In fact, however, IW service seems to do just the opposite. Most IWs report that they suffer with identity issues when they move to a new country, become aware of just how far short their Christian walk actually falls, and discover more personal issues that need to be resolved than when they are in their home country. If an IW is motivated to serve because of any of these variables, I would recommend that they not be sent to +P countries. +P countries need IWs who already have firmly established identities and have few internal conflicts that need to be resolved.

Because of the importance of motivation in mediating stress, I recommend it should be included in the screening of candidates who wish to serve as IWs in +P contexts. Some of the specific areas that should be assessed in a screening include:

Are there any indications that this person is motivated for overseas service because they:

1.) Don't have anything else to do or can't keep a job?

2.) Are avoiding a bad family or social situation in their home country?

3.) Are trying to "find" themselves or resolve some internal conflicts?

During screening, the person assessing the individual can provide a yes or no answer to each of these questions. Many techniques can be employed to help answer these questions, but the most helpful one is likely to be an interview where the candidate is provided opportunities to talk about why they want to be an IW in a +P context. Questions about their family situation and work experience can also be asked.

Positive answers to any of these questions should not necessarily be viewed as immediate grounds to not accept a candidate. However, they can help provide a better picture of the person's overall functioning. For example, I would be much more concerned about a candidate who has a history of depression if they are motivated to serve overseas because their home country family situation is so dysfunctional than I would be for the same person whose only motivation to go overseas is to please God and who will miss family, job and life in their home country.

Married Couples

Any married couple who has served overseas will confess that the stressors they encounter stretch their marriage relationship unlike anything they have experienced prior to service. A strong marital foundation is, therefore, necessary for couples who want to serve overseas, especially in +P contexts.

Assessing marital health can employ many of the same techniques that are used in assessing individual mental health - standardized testing, history and interview. There are many good standardized tests that assess marital health, such as the Marital Satisfaction Inventory (MSI). This 150 question self-administered test assesses marital strength on a variety of empirically derived scales and provides a comprehensive assessment of possible areas of conflict in the marriage. Couples who are highly dissatisfied or have intense areas of conflict will likely struggle in devastating ways once they encounter the stress of life and service overseas. At a minimum, these couples should be referred for marital therapy from a reputable and professional therapist prior to being deployed.

A history of the marriage should answer the following questions, which I view as similar to the "fleshly vulnerabilities" discussed in the previous section:

Is there a history of legal separations?

Is there a history of extramarital affairs?

Is there a history of martial counseling, treatment or therapy?

When assessing historical struggles in a marriage, I recommend using the same rule-of-thumb that we discussed in the previous section on assessing fleshly vulnerabilities. Specifically, I don't recommend ruling out a couple who has had significant struggles in the past, but I believe you can estimate that there still remains a 65% chance that the couple will return to their most disastrous times when they encounter the extreme stress of +P service. For example, if a couple has experienced an intense conflict that required them to seek marital therapy five years ago, my experience suggests that, even though this conflict hasn't been a major issue for them for five years, there is a 65% chance that they will return to a similar condition and need similar interventions when they encounter the stress of +P service.

Children

Issues with children's health, educational needs, or emotional problems ranks second to team problems in the list of most common reasons why IWs leave the field early. Raising children in any overseas situation is demanding for parents. Raising children in a +P context is extremely difficult and stressful. Raising children with special emotional, learning, or behavioral needs in a +P context is practically impossible and extremely stressful for both the child and the family. The stress on the child is particularly troubling as they often are unable to obtain the psychological, education or medical help that is needed for healthy development. Many childhood problems that can easily be treated and managed in the home country become major issues when exacerbated by the stress of +P service, and in the worst-case scenarios, can lead to long-term emotional or adjustment problems in the child and family.

Because of the double jeopardy of lack of services and high stress levels, I do not feel it is appropriate to send families with special needs children to most +P locations. There is too much risk that the child will sustain emotional damage and that the family will collapse under the stress to justify sending special needs children to these types of situations. Screening of family applicants, therefore, should also include some assessment of the children's needs.

Screening of children can be accomplished by collecting historical data on the child(ren)'s educational and emotional functioning and by employing a standardized assessment scale (such as the Behavioral Assessment System for Children or the Child Behavioral Checklist). These easy to administer and score scales use self-report (for older children), parental, and teacher ratings to provide an assessment of the child's emotional and behavioral functioning. In addition, a child's educational achievement can be measured using a number of computer-based achievement tests (such as the Basic Achievement Skills Inventory) which compare a child's current knowledge base and academic skills to peers their age. These tests serve as a good screening method for academic struggles and possible learning disabilities. If data from the interview or the objective assessment methods suggest the possibility of problems, then I recommend a more formal assessment, including an intellectual assessment and clinical interview.

Whatever screening method is chosen, the screening should provide answers to the following questions:

Is there any indication that the child(ren) might need a more thorough psychological assessment to rule out severe behavioral, emotional or educational needs?

Will the child(ren)likely have special educational needs due to learning or behavioral struggles or physical conditions?

❧ 2 ❧

PRE-FIELD TRAINING

Our goal in supporting IWs who serve in +P contexts is to provide them with unequivocal support, support that is not mixed with a need to evaluate the nature or etiology of problems that come up. In this model, any problems that arise are viewed as stress reactions and not as indicative of underlying psychological, spiritual or motivational issues. Being able to view any struggle that arises as a stress reaction provides IWs with a great deal of resilience as they serve in high stress areas. Adequate screening procedures, as we have just seen, are an important part in setting the groundwork for providing this kind of support.

In this section, I will also propose that pre-field training plays an important part in establishing this type of support system. The type of training that I envision as necessary is not the normal training that SOs provide to their IWs. As I have argued throughout this book, most SOs provide very good training for things like cultural adjustment, learning languages, functioning on a team, and doing cross-cultural ministry. The thing that SOs often neglect, however, is dealing with deep, heart-related issues that allow stress to empower flesh. The training that I propose IWs who will serve in +P contexts undergo would be an additional course that specifically targets these areas. This course would be a certification training where anyone who completes it is viewed as qualified or certified to serve in +P settings. It is presented to the IWs as specialized preparations that only people serving in hazardous settings are required to participate in. IWs who choose not to complete this training will not be able to serve in +P countries. Those that do will show they possesses sufficient motivation, tools and skills to deal with factors that hinder their relationship with God, empower their flesh, or damage their team relationships. The trade-off for undergoing this intense training is that the IW will grow in their relationship with God as they deal with heart related issues. They will also learn many skills that will equip them at a deeper level for effective ministry and to ward off spiritual and psychological attacks.

Two analogies can clarify the type of training I'm envisioning and how it will enable SOs to provide nonjudgmental support to their IWs. The first analogy is that of an astronaut. Astronauts represent the most highly qualified, well trained, emotionally stable individuals in the aeronautical community. Once an astronaut candidate passes all the physical and emotional training requirements and earns their astronaut wings, they are certified as qualified to do one of the most dangerous and stressful jobs on (and off) the planet. If during a mission, an astronaut develops an emotional or physical reaction, no one assumes that this is anything other than a stress reaction for someone who is being pushed to their emotional and physical limits. No one questions the qualifications, training or motivation of an astronaut.

Because of the rigorous screening and training of astronauts, the space agency can provide them with unequivocal support. Astronauts are the pride and joy of the country they serve and need nothing from the space agency but support to do the job they are sent to do. No one would think to rate an astronaut's motivation, fitness or professional proficiency on a one to ten-point scale in order to improve them and give them performance feedback. The astronaut's training program already ensures that they are fit, motivated and proficient at the highest possible level. Because these factors are no longer an issue, the space agency can provide the astronaut with the unequivocal support they need. The space agency's support role, therefore, becomes one of monitoring the astronaut's stress level and providing support as necessary.

The second analogy is that of military special forces training. Serving in the Special Forces is a high honor and only those individuals who meet the strictest screening standards and pass through the most intensive and grueling training programs are accepted into the Special Forces. Those who are selected have proven that they are physically and emotionally prepared to handle the special authority and weapons that they are assigned. The training they undergo proves to the soldier and their leaders that the soldier possesses all the physical and emotional stamina they will need to carry out the stressful special missions that they will be assigned to.

Do Special Forces soldiers develop emotional problems when serving in combat? Of course they do; but no one thinks that these problems are anything other than stress reactions that happen while they are engaged in very difficult and dangerous missions. No one would say that a Navy SEAL, for example, has a stress reaction because they are weak or unmotivated. They would say that the SEAL developed the stress reaction because the demands of combat are so extreme. Likewise, no one tasked with supporting a Navy SEAL wonders how a SEAL needs to be improved. They don't need improvement; they need the support, equipment and empowerment to do what they are highly trained and motivated to do.

In my opinion, I think only the astronauts and Special Forces operatives of the Christian community should be sent to serve in +P countries as IWs. This recommendation is not because I believe that these people will be more successful in these kinds of assignments, or that they are better Christians than their peers. Rather, I make this recommendation because **I believe that people who are screened, trained and certified as ready for +P service are in the best position to manage the intense stress, spiritual attacks, and stress-empowered flesh issues that they will encounter.** This will help them have longevity of service and be less likely to develop ministry and team-damaging emotional reactions. In addition, when a SO screens, trains, and certifies IWs in this way, it will change the way they can and should support these IWs while serving. It will change the member care model to one where unequivocal support is the milieu of the support program.

+P Certification Training

In modern wars, beyond a minimal level of physical fitness and technical learning of how to fight, the soldier's most important training is in social-psychological reaction patterns... and the bonding with a group for accomplishing the military mission. [1]

-War Psychiatry Manual

My impression is that most SOs excel in preparing their IWs with the technical learning they will need to serve overseas. For many IW assignments, this type of training proves adequate. However, given the intensity of the stress associated with +P service, IWs who plan to serve in these countries need additional training - training that teaches them how to deal with the "social-psychological reaction patterns" they will have. As the military has discovered, in high stress combat environments, how a soldier deals with their emotional, social and psychological reactions is actually more important for military success and the overall health of the soldier than weapons proficiency or level of physical fitness. It seems prudent, therefore, that IWs who plan to serve in +P countries should receive additional training that will help prepare them for these factors and help build team cohesiveness that mediate the stress they will experience.

Before we look specifically at how training to address psychological issues and team cohesion might look, I might add here that the type of "social-psychological reaction patterns" that IWs experience in +P service are different than soldiers serving in combat. For soldiers, these reaction patterns often involve dealing with trauma, overt fear, and aggressive impulses. For IWs, however, these reaction patterns often touch on spiritual and heart issues that lead to fleshly vulnerabilities. Though the type of reaction patterns between IWs and soldiers are different, the two groups do share one commonality: It is often these emotionally based issues that result in psychological and spiritual breakdown during service, not some lack of intellectual or technical preparation. **One of the important theses of this book series is that stress empowers flesh, and that IWs need training and support to effectively address the stress-empowered flesh issues that they will encounter during service in +P settings.**

We will now turn to a discussion of what training to address these emotional/psychological/spiritual reaction patterns can look like. In this section, I'll present an overview of how what I refer to as +P Certification Training should seek to accomplish, it's general goals and parameters, and its rationale. I will then present an actual training program that can be used to accomplish these goals.

The first aspect of +P certification training is that it should be required in addition to all other training that the SO typically provides its IWs. This training is devised and billed as necessary only to persons who want to serve in +P countries where they need special training to deal with the intense stress they will encounter. It should be presented as test-like in nature and, if successfully completed, lead to certification to serve in +P countries. IWs who are not willing or able to complete the training can still be considered by the SO for deployment in non +P settings, but they are required to successfully complete it if they wish to serve in the high stress environments of +P countries. Again, the analogy of Navy SEAL training is appropriate. Normal soldiers can serve with dignity and honor in their individual units. However, those who aspire to the extra responsibility, prestige and authority of a Navy SEAL, must successfully complete SEAL training after their initial basic training. Chronologically, +P certification training, like special forces training, should be the last step in the IW's pre-field training process.

Second, +P Certification Training should challenge the IW to examine flesh and fleshly vulnerabilities in a new way. One primary purpose is to teach the IW to understand how stress becomes a spiritual battle that can be overcome by employing spiritual solutions. The IW should understand that participation in the +P training will require him or her to look inside at their emotional reaction patterns that may cause them to be vulnerable to stress and flesh, and which may contribute to team issues.

It is important to note that all IWs who participate in the +P certification course have already undergone psychological screening. The reason this is important is that the exercises in +P training may provoke strong emotional reactions (possibly depression) in people who have substantial unresolved trauma history. Psychological screening should be accomplished before +P training to ensure that each individual can handle the stress that dealing with their emotional issues will entail. A psychologist or mental health professional should be consulted if there is question about a person's suitability to undergo the stress of +P certification training or if they develop intense emotional reactions during the course.

Even though +P training is stressful for the participants, the benefits it provides to the IW and SOs are worth the cost. These benefits include:

1.) The screening and additional training will allow reactions that IWs have while serving overseas to be viewed as normal stress reactions that happen in highly qualified people serving in very difficult places. Viewing struggles as normal stress responses builds spiritual and emotional resiliency, which will help the IW serve longer and more effectively.

Viewing struggles as a normal stress response also makes it easier for the SO to provide the unequivocal support that is so needed by IWs in +P contexts. Because the IW has been screened, trained, and has demonstrated their willingness to deal with flesh and heart issues by completing +P Certification Training, the SO and MCP won't question the reason for the IW's struggles. They won't wonder if there is an unidentified mental health issue, or a lack of motivation, or spiritual immaturity. Rather, the MCP and SO can, with confidence, can provide non-evaluative support. Non-evaluative support is also an important component of building spiritual and emotional resiliency.

2.) +P Certification Training will set the stage for the future support program that the SO will use for IWs serving in +P contexts. Not only will the +P training allow the MCPs to provide nonevaluative support, it will also teach a common vernacular that can be employed by all when stress reactions are encountered. +P certification training has the goal of teaching a common way to understand stress reactions and presents a model that is known by the MCP, SO and IW for how stress reactions will be understood and supported. Everyone, for example, will be able to understand what is meant when the MCP asks the IW, "What is happening in your low road right now?[2]". This common vernacular will help to normalize both the reaction the IW is having, and the support program employed by the SO.

3.) Unfortunately, service in +P countries places individuals at higher risk to be victims of crime, traffic accidents, persecution, violence or terror attacks. +P Certification training also proactively prepares IWs for the unthinkable. Though these events are extremely traumatic, research suggests that providing some preparation for what to expect and how to handle the emotional turmoil that these events entail is helpful for long-term recovery.

+P Certification Training also provides proactive methods to help with team conflicts. Team members, who have all gone through the screening and +P training, are more willing to give grace to each other. This is because team conflicts can rightfully be attributed to the stress of the assignment and not to an underlying weakness or personality disorder. Team members will also have a specific plan that they have all agreed to beforehand to implement during times of conflict or stress.

This plan emphasizes concrete ways they can get along by dying to self and reaching for spiritual solutions to their conflicts

4.) An obvious goal of +P Certification training is for the IWs to identify stress-empowered flesh issues and be able to deal with them. Stress-empowered flesh has to do with automatic emotional response tendencies and drives which lead to spiritual vulnerabilities and relational conflicts. Dealing with these vulnerabilities often requires teaching new ways to understand and deal with the emotional and personality issues that IWs bring to service with them. +P Certification training provides many of the same types of interventions used in psychotherapy to help accomplish these goals. +P training will also help identify if further professional intervention is needed before individuals deploy to their assignments.

5.) And finally, +P Certification Training focuses on equipping the IW for the spiritual battles that accompany +P service. An important component of this is teaching new ways to humbly rely on God's grace. Titus 2:11-12[3] is a key verse in understanding the role that grace plays in empowering people to live righteous lives, lives where they are less vulnerable to flesh. According to this passage, it is grace that trains us to reject godless ways. +P certification training provides a model for how grace brings about these changes and encourages IWs to let their stress-empowered flesh issues experience God's grace in life-giving ways.

Real-Life Team Bonding

The last part of the pre-field preparation process for people who plan to serve in +P contexts is developing team bonding and cohesion. Unit cohesion and team bonding are extremely important in high stress assignments. In fact, military research has identified that unit cohesion and team bonding are the best mediators of combat stress in combat units.[4] Combat veterans consistently report that the relationship they have with other soldiers in their unit is the primary motivator that allows them to continue in battle and not run away in the face of danger.

SOs also recognize the importance of good team relationships and bonding and they attempt to create it in many ways. The best method for creating team bonding and unit cohesion, however, is not the team building exercises that are often employed. Rather, the best team bonding and cohesion occurs when a team or unit mutually accomplishes shared stressful experiences. **Teams bond best when they are challenged with real-world stressors, not concocted exercises designed to get to know each other or understand each other's personality.**

The military also knows the advantage of providing a stress-filled training experience for their troops. Much of the abuse that is heaped on new recruits, the physical and emotional challenges that they face in training, are specifically designed to inoculate them to the stress of combat that they will later experience. For example, when a drill Sergeant yells abusive words in the face of a recruit, they are intentionally working to inoculate the soldier from the effects of the hatred the enemy will hurl on him or her during combat. For the soldier to learn that they can still function effectively even in the face of such overt hatred and abuse provides them with a psychological inoculation for the future abuse they will suffer when attacked by their enemy in combat.

Before individuals serve on teams in +P countries, I think that it is prudent to have them undergo inoculation towards the types of stressors that commonly occur on teams in IW service. The last stage of a training and preparation program, therefore, should include a stressful team exercise that the group can accomplish together. As the teams are going through these stressful exercises, their MCP can provide them with daily debriefings and opportunities to apply the stress reducing techniques that were learned in their certification training. It is important, however, that the stressful activities that the team undertakes have real-world meaning and are not just concocted meaningless undertakings, which will lead only to frustration. Two examples of appropriate inoculation activities include a week or two of intensive language learning, and a week or two of work practicums.

One of the team building activities we are implementing in the organization I work for is to have all of our teams go to a +P country and participate in a week-long intensive class where they learn to read and pronounce Arabic. They will also learn a few simple phrases that are commonly used in all Muslim countries. Although some of the countries where our workers serve do not speak Arabic as their primary language, the Arabic language is such an integral part of Islam that learning the alphabet and some simple phrases will be helpful in most settings. This makes learning the Arabic alphabet a real-world, meaningful task and not just a concocted team building activity.

Learning to read and write Arabic in a week's time is also a challenging endeavor which should evoke the feelings of helplessness, competition, and self-doubt that are commonly experienced on teams serving in +P countries. As the team encounters these common stress reactions, their MCP can normalize them and help them become aware of the expectations and cognitive processes that are related to them. These will have already been taught to the IWs in the certification training and they can be reinforced and applied to help resolve this real-life stressful situation. Special focus can also be given to identifying and rooting out destructive team dynamics that arise under stress.

Another example of a suitable real-world team bonding situation is a teaching practicum. For example, one teaching organization that I consult with requires all their teachers to receive a TEFL (Teaching English as a Foreign Language) certificate before they serve overseas. One requirement for obtaining this certification is that the teachers must do a practicum where their teaching is observed and critiqued. If this practicum took place in a +P country where the IWs were teaching real students in a real classroom setting, it would be an excellent team bonding activity, especially if all the teachers observed each other. This type of teaching practicum is sufficiently stressful to illicit the feelings of competition, helplessness and frustration so that these can be processed and then inoculated against. After successfully working through these feelings in a real-world stressful environment, they should have less effect on the IW when they are again encountered after deployment.

Practically, it will be hard for the people who will be deployed on a team together to be classmates in the exact same real-life team building experience. Some people may ask, therefore, how this would build team relationships. The answer is that the team-building experience can be a shared experience among all IWs in the organization, even if people do not go through it simultaneously. For example, imagine that one person will be joining a team who is serving in Yemen. The existing team has already been there three years. The common experience of all the team members having gone through the same team-building activity of learning the Arabic alphabet, having learned the same system for walking through their stress responses, will serve as a team bonding experience even though it didn't happen at the same time. The new team can talk about how hard learning to say the *Qaaf* sound, for example, was, and they can commiserate about how they felt so much slower at catching on to Arabic than their classmates. All the team members will also know that each one has successfully completed this difficult task and was willing to appropriately process the emotional toll and relationship stress related to the task, building mutual respect and trust. So, even if the experience is not shared temporally, it can still be a bonding experience that will help with team cohesion.

✿ 3 ✿

CREATING TRUST

Trust Between the MCP and the IW

The screening and training methods we have just discussed are designed to set the foundation for SOs to provide IWs with unequivocal support while serving in +P countries. They are designed in order that SOs and MCPs can correctly diagnose any struggles that IWs have as stress related – not because of an unidentified mental health condition, lack of motivation, or spiritual immaturity. Proper attribution of a problem's cause is important as it will determine how the MCP and SO care for the struggling person. If the problems are because of stress, then nonevaluative support can be offered. If, however, the cause is determined to be lack of motivation, or an underlying mental health issue, support becomes more administrative as the SO and MCP look for ways to ameliorate the underlying issues.

In addition to building a foundation where SOs and MCPs can provide IWs with nonjudgmental support, member care programs also need to build trust between the MCP and the IW. This allows the IW the safety to address their struggles and weaknesses, decreasing the impacts of these on their emotional and spiritual health. A safe relationship like this often requires some level of confidentiality. Likewise, there needs to be a measure of trust established between the MCP and the SO. SOs need to be assured that issues that violate policy or are damaging to Kingdom work are being addressed in appropriate ways.

The balance between creating a safe place where IWs can talk to their MCPs about any struggle they have, versus the SO's need to know, is a tricky one. However, I believe there are some ways that this balance can be achieved. In the following section I will present some concrete steps that can be taken to balance these two needs. Let's first look at ways to create trust between the IW and the MCP.

Underlying Attitude: Struggles Come from Stress, not Failure

After IWs have completed the +P Certification Training program, they should be well indoctrinated with the idea that the SO has certified them as qualified and ready to serve in hazardous places. The SO should have also given the IW the message that, since they are qualified, certified, and healthy, the purpose of the member care program is to support the IW - not to evaluate, motivate or improve him or her.

As I've previously outlined, a good analogy for the kind of support that the SO needs to provide IWs is similar to how astronauts are supported. Astronauts have gone through intense screening and training programs and are the best of the best in the aeronautical profession. When they go on a mission, their support staff's responsibility is not to improve or correct them. It is not to try to motivate them to do better. Rather, the support staff's only goal is to monitor the astronaut and provide for him or her the support they need to successfully complete the mission they have been sent on. No one thinks to rate an astronaut's performance on a 1 to 5 scale and then work to improve their scores. The astronaut's only limitations are his or her physical and intellectual limits, and these have already been conditioned to their peak. If an astronaut develops a problem or struggle, it means that the stress they have been under has pushed them to their limit. No one blames the astronaut for having limits; instead, they work to decrease the stress level or provide other ways for the astronaut to compensate. Another way to think of this support arrangement is that astronauts only receive medals for the dangerous and risky jobs they do, never reprimands.

I suggest that IWs serving in +P contexts need "astronaut-like" support. They need to be assured that, no matter how they struggle, they will receive medals and not reprimands. As with astronauts, IWs need to have the message reinforced to them that any struggle that happens while they are serving is because of the stressful job they are doing. Since fear of being negatively evaluated is one of the primary reasons IWs do not seek help from MCPs, they need this kind of astronaut-like support to feel safe enough to openly address their struggle with their MCPs.

One more analogy of the support program I am recommending is that of a wounded soldier. If a soldier is wounded in battle, no one will blame the soldier. The reason the soldier falls is because he has an enemy that is fighting against him and trying to kill him. The role I'm suggesting a MCP serve in +P countries is that of a combat medic. A medic runs to the wounded soldier and gets him or her the help that is needed. The medic doesn't look for ways to correct or improve the soldier; and later, the soldier's commanding officer (the SO leadership) will even give the soldier a Purple Heart medal for sustaining an injury in battle.

With appropriate training and screening, I think we can treat the struggles that IWs have as combat wounds rather than moral failings. The battle that IWs fight is not one of physical struggles; it is a battle against the flesh and against the powers of darkness. The injuries sustained will be spiritual and moral, and not necessarily physical. When an IW struggles, he or she needs to know that their MCP will meet these struggles by normalizing them and attributing them to attacks of the enemy. This will allow the seeds of trust to grow between the MCP and the IW.

Normalizing

The concept of normalizing is very important in psychotherapy. Normalizing essentially means that you tell the individual that the response they are having is a normal reaction to the difficulties they have experienced (or are experiencing) in life. The reason why they are depressed, for example, is a normal response to the helpless situations they have experienced. The simple process of helping the person accept that their response is understandable and normal is extremely therapeutic.

The military has learned this lesson for combat stress. The basic model for treating those who are overwhelmed by their combat experiences is to tell them that their responses, whatever they are, are normal stress reactions. This simple intervention has profound effects. We now know that most aspects of emotional responses happen unconsciously and involuntarily and are mediated by the part of the brain called the limbic system. When a soldier is overwhelmed by combat stress, his limbic system has initiated an unconscious and automatic self-protective response. When the limbic system initiates this response, another part of the soldier's brain, the cortex, tries to make sense of what is happening. If the cortex decides that the self-protective response is because of weakness or cowardice, then the soldier has a good chance of becoming a psychiatric casualty; they believe that their emotional response shows their weakness and lack of worth. However, if the soldier hears from a respected mental health professional that his or her automatic response is normal, the soldier's cortex can latch on to this explanation and the limbic system's response will no longer be as troubling, damaging, or as able to dictate their responses.

Some people object to the idea of normalizing because they fear it will limit personal responsibility. If a soldier says, for example, that "my horror in combat is just a normal response", then the concern is that the soldier will no longer want to push him or herself to fight, but rather wallow in their fear response. Likewise, if a depressed person understands their depression as a normal response to their helplessness inducing experiences from childhood, will they not feel that they have no choice but to be depressed and helpless? Might they say, "I'm right to be depressed, so don't try to help me change?"

Research into psychotherapy and the neurosciences paints a different picture, however. Normalizing, by teaching about what is going on in the brain during an emotional response, doesn't lead to a lack of ability or motivation to change. Rather, once an individual understands the underlying processes that are driving their emotional responses, they have more control over their emotions and are less likely to be determined by unconscious and automatic brain systems. Normalizing also decreases self-loathing and shame, two factors that are known to decrease motivation and ability to change.

Once people begin to understand their responses are normal, they can begin to take on a new attitude towards their problem. Daniel Siegel describes this attitude as this problem is "not my fault, but it is my responsibility[1]." Combat stress reactions, because they are normal brain reactions that are initiated by unconscious and automatic limbic system responses, are not the soldier's fault. He or she should not feel shame for these. However, these responses are still his or her responsibility. Since they have control over how they view their responses, they can choose to limit how their automatic emotional responses will determine their future.

Likewise, the depressed person's limbic system's responses are not his or her fault; they are automatic responses triggered by neurochemical reactions and stress hormones. However, neuroscience research also teaches us that the depressed person still has responsibility for his or her reactions. This responsibility comes because we know that there are things that a depressed person can do to change his or her automatic responses. The depressed person, even though not at fault for their brain's normal depressive reactions, is not helpless to change them and does not need to be controlled by them.

I spend so much time on this idea of normalizing because it is important in helping IWs deal with struggles. If an IW, for example, struggles with looking at pornography, what is the best way to deal with this? Should the MCP and the SO try to use consequences and shame to motivate change in the IW? Most MCPs know that this is not the best method. However, many of the procedures that I've seen SOs and MCPs use in these situations send the unconscious message that the IW is to blame for a "moral failing".

I think a better way to help this IW is to normalize the response and to help him or her understand that the struggle with pornography is not their fault; it is their responsibility, however. The struggle is not their fault because it is a stress-empowered flesh issue - a normal flesh response in this individual when overwhelmed by stress. The struggle

HAMILTON T. BURKE, PH.D.

remains their responsibility, however, since there are things (both spiritually and psychologically) that the IW can do to not be controlled by these automatic responses.

The response that I'm advocating is the same one Jesus used when dealing with the woman caught in adultery.[2] Jesus uses a two-pronged method to empower this woman to overcome her sins. The first of these was to take the power away from the system that wanted to condemn her. The system was set up so that the woman was responsible for her "moral failing" and deserved punishment. Too often, SOs have the same attitude, that "moral failings" are things that need to be punished. Jesus, however, breaks down this system by showing that we are all "moral failures", just like the woman, and should be punished.

After breaking down the guilt and shame system of those who wanted to condemn the adulterous woman, Jesus turns his focus on her, and the way he treats her is very revealing about how people change morally. Jesus doesn't tell her to first clean up her act or he will condemn her. What he says is "I don't condemn you", and I've taken care of the system that does. In a sense, Jesus normalizes her struggles and sin as part of the human condition. He essentially tells her that he understands her sins are a fleshly reaction that are not her fault. After normalizing her sins, however, Jesus turns to the second prong of his approach to her. He tells her that she has power to go and sin no more. Jesus says to her that her sin is not her fault and that she is forgiven for them, but that her future reactions are still her responsibility. Jesus seems to teach us in this interaction that the process of wiping away shame and guilt, the normalizing process, gives us the power to go and sin no more.

Approaching struggling IWs in this way will not only increase the IW's ability to go and sin no more, but it will have the added benefit of increasing trust between the MCP and the IW. If the IW knows that the MCP will not blame or shame them for struggles, that struggles will be normalized, they are much more likely to openly discuss them with their MCP. Perfect love drives out fear[3], and the normalizing of the IW's struggle helps him or her trust their MCP. Having the IW bring their struggles into the IW/MCP relationship will keep them from suffering alone and hiding their issues. If issues and struggles are hidden and away from the Body's ability to support, then the devil can wreak havoc on the IW's life and ministry.

MCP vs. Support Leader

If the SO and member care program adopts the astronaut support model, then the role of the MCP changes drastically. The MCP no longer will have the coaching, mentoring/evaluation role that many SOs place them in. Rather, the MCP will take on more of a monitoring and support role. The astronaut model of member care that I'm describing here is designed for those serving in +P, hazardous contexts. It is likely that it will not be suitable for supporting IWs who have not gone through the added screening and training that +P certified individuals have.

As SOs consider changing the role of their MCPs to more of a support role, they may find that changing the name of the MCP will be useful.[4] One term that I think captures more of the idea I have for this role is Support Leader. The title Support Leader suggests to the IW that the person's role is to support them by leading. I envision the Support Leader as a person who has leadership authority over the IW (and possibly the whole team). However, the authority they have is to support the IW and team as they accomplish the task the SO leadership gives them. The Support Leader, therefore, is a mid-level leader that provides the support needed for the IW to do their job.

Remember, the +P certified IW is viewed as healthy, motivated and as the cream of the crop of the IW world. They do not need their immediate leaders to improve them or motivate them to do better work; they only need them to provide the monitoring and support that will assist them as they do their very demanding and stressful work. The Support Leader, therefore, is seen as a mid-level leader between the SO leadership (who give assignments) and the IW/team. They are tasked with helping the IW and team accomplish their assignments, and they do this by providing unequivocal support, by normalizing any struggles that the IW's face, by supporting the IW as they deal with stress-empowered flesh issues, and by arranging and coordinating any logistical or other support that is needed.

Part of the monitoring/supporting role that Support Leaders have is to maintain frequent contact with the people under their support leadership. Support Leaders are not the typical MCPs who come for a visit once or twice a year and send encouraging WhatsApp[5] messages every-so-often. Being a Support Leader is a full-time position that requires frequent interaction with and monitoring of the IW. Applying the astronaut support model again, the Support Leader would be the individual who is monitoring the astronaut's vital signs and behavior during a spacewalk to be able to suggest to both the astronaut and the mission commander when the IW needs to return to the space station for rest and recovery.

To facilitate the monitoring aspect of the Support Leader's role, I recommend that the IW provide weekly feedback on the level of stress they are experiencing in several different areas. I have created a short Excel spreadsheet that facilitates a quick and easy overview of the IW's weekly functioning in several key areas. For example, on this spreadsheet the IW will provide ratings (from -10 to +10) about how stressful or positive variables like their finances, security/safety, team relationships, work assignment, purity issues, and marriage/family life are. There is also a place for them to rate their overall stress level for the week (on a 1 - 10 scale). The scale only takes about three minutes to fill out and email back to the IW's Support Leader each week. The completed form allows the Support Leader to have a quick glance into how the IW is functioning and in what areas they might need additional support.[6]

Support Leaders can use the weekly reports the IWs send to facilitate communication about struggles the IW may be having. For example, if an IW has a low score on the Purity Scale for the week, the Support Leader may inquire about what support they need in this area and how they can be praying for the IW. Likewise, if the IW reports a negative score on team, the Support Leader may wish to follow up on this to see how the team could be encouraged or supported.

One aspect related to building trust between the MCP (or, Support Leader as I'm referring to them here) and the IW is worth mentioning here. I strongly encourage the role of Support Leader be done by someone serving in the general region of the people they are leading.

Many IWs report it is hard for them to trust MCPs who do not live in the same region where they are working. MCPs who live in North America, for example, and come on a bi-annual visit to the IWs will lack many of the shared experiences and won't necessarily understand the stressors at a level necessary to relate to the IW.

One IW I talked with was bemoaning that his MCP, who lives in North America and comes to visit him twice a year, makes things worse when he visits. "My MCP has hobbies, a nice car back in the States, owns a home, has lots of friends, good free schools for his kids, a large supportive church, and dental insurance. He represents everything I've given up to serve overseas, and seeing him happy and excited when he comes to visit is like rubbing salt into my raw wounds." Arrangements like this make it hard for the IW to trust the MCP; the IW feels the MCP judges them using North American eyes. My recommendation to SOs, therefore, is that the Support Leader should live in the same region as those they support.

The Support Leader position, as envisioned in this model, is filled by an IW who is also living and working to further the Kingdom in a +P context. The only difference between the Support Leader and the IWs they are supporting is their work assignment; the Support Leader's primary job is supporting those in their care. Because of the intensity of the interactions between Support Leaders and IWs, I recommend a ratio of about ten to fifteen IWs to every Support Leader. Ideally, the Support Leader should also be someone who has several years' experience as an IW in a +P assignment before they take on the Support Leader role.

Limited Confidentiality and Nonevaluative Support

Two of the major stumbling blocks in creating trust between the MCP and the IW are the issues of confidentiality and evaluation. For all parties involved, there is great benefit if the IW can freely discuss his or her issues and struggles in a safe relationship where there is no fear of evaluation. For the IW, this provides much needed support in an environment where support is a valuable commodity. For the MCP, this opens opportunity to provide the help and support they want to give. And for the SO, the openness of the IW allows it to ensure that everyone is healthy, and that there are no secret sins or bombshells hiding below the surface ready to sink the organization.

While in the perfect world, IWs would be completely open with everyone about any struggles that they are having, reality is quite different. Because the areas where IWs usually need the most support from their MCP involve personal struggles, struggles that are embarrassing and shameful, struggles that could possibly make others wonder about their fitness for continued IW service, they find it difficult to discuss these with anyone who has the authority over their future career or service. MCPs who are closely related to organization leadership structure often find that IWs are unwilling to discuss much with them. However, SOs who have MCPs who are separate from their organizational leadership wonder if their members are having secret, destructive problems that they need to know about.

While I'm writing this section, I'm consulting with a SO about their MC program. This SO's director of MC spoke with me extensively about how this issue of confidentiality affects her MCPs as they attempt to care for the IWs under them. She complained that the biggest obstacle faced by her MCPs is that the IWs don't want to openly talk about their struggles and issues. The IWs fear that the MCP will judge, ridicule or negatively evaluate them if they confess their struggles to them. One of the reasons driving this response is that the SO also requires their MCPs to perform an evaluative function with the IWs. After each visit with an IW, the MCP files reports to the SO leadership about how the IW is doing. In MC arrangements like this, it is not surprising that IWs feel the need to screen what they say to their MCPs.

One important step SOs can take to lessen this problem is to grant a limited degree of confidentiality between the IW and the MCP. This confidentiality is not the legally binding type set up in a professional counseling or legal relationship; however, some guarantee that the MCP's purpose of interacting with the IW is not to evaluate them, and that, within limits, the MCP will provide privacy to the IW should be given. An informed consent form that clearly describes the desire to give privacy, and the times when this privacy will be broken by the

MCP without the IW's permission, may be helpful to present to the IW prior to the initiation of their relationship with their MCP. Here is a sample of excerpts from a form that I have devised for this very purpose:

> Your support leader is available to assist you in resolving any issue that prevents you from being effective in your overseas service. We understand that privacy is an important part of the trust needed to build a relationship where any issues that hinders your service can be discussed. To the best of our ability, we want to provide you with a place where you can freely talk without undue fear that it will negatively affect your standing with (your sending organization). We want to provide you with assurance that what you discuss with your Support Leader will not be casually shared with family, friends, leadership or your teammates.

> There are some situations, however, where your Support Leader is obligated to break the privacy of the relationship with you and inform appropriate leadership or civil authorities about the content of your discussions or your behaviors. We want to inform you of these beforehand so that you know the limits of the privacy in your relationship with your Support Leader before you begin your relationship with him or her.

> Your SL is obligated to inform (your Sending Organization) leadership and/or civil authorities under the following circumstance:

> - If you pose a danger to yourself or others.
> - If there is (or suspected) abuse, neglect or exploitation of others (children, elders, nationals).
> - Illegal conduct.
> - Intractable team conflict or relationship issues.
> - Emotional or mental health conditions that significantly affect your ability to function on a team or in your host country (even if you do not pose a threat to self or other's safety).

- Violations of your Sending Organizations policies or code of conduct.
- Other situations as deemed necessary by your Support Leader.

Everyone would agree that some trust in the IW/MCP relationship is necessary. This begs the question, however, why many SOs find it difficult to give the privacy necessary to establish this kind of relationship, why these SOs place an evaluative role on their MCPs. There are, of course, many factors related to this decision, and finding the balance between the need to know and the need for confidentiality is difficult.

One of the main reasons I have found for including evaluation in the MCP's role is based on a faulty understanding of how people change. The evaluation model of change believes that struggles express some area that needs correction, mentoring or motivation in order to change. In this model, positive changes in a person's life happen because the negative evaluation motivates them to take seriously the issue and to make appropriate changes. However, while this theory of change may work for some situations, I do not think it fits into our "astronaut support" model of member care. Astronauts do not need to be motivated. Any issues they encounter are because they are pushed to their physical and emotional limits, not because they lack motivation or concern. In fact, for people attempting to accomplish dangerous and difficult tasks, evaluation hinders their ability to adequately perform. The fear of humiliation and failure can lead to a self-doubt and timidity.

I think the Apostle Paul understands that evaluation is not always the best way to motivate people. Two sections out of 1 Thessalonians chapter 4 illustrate this point well. The first comes from verse 1. Here Paul says:

Finally then, brothers and sisters, we ask you and urge you in the Lord Jesus, that as you received instruction from us about how you must live and please God (as you are in fact living) that you do so more and more.[7]

In this section, Paul does not say something like: "In my report back to the elders in the Jerusalem church, I'm going to note that you are only at a 5 or 6 on the living a godly life scale. I will also document that we have discussed ways to improve your score, and that we hope you will be in the 8 or 9 range by next summer." Rather, Paul says (my paraphrase), "You are already living up to the instructions that we have given you about leading a godly life. Good job! Do this more and more."

A similar passage is found further down in chapter 4 (verses 9-10).[8] In this section Paul is talking about brotherly love. He uses the same formula for encouraging them as he did in verse 1 when he says (my paraphrase), "God has already taught you how to love each other, and you're doing a great job already. We want to encourage you to do this more and more."

In both passages, Paul starts with the understanding that the Thessalonians are already equipped, motivated and trained to live a godly life full of brotherly love, and they are already doing well. They are like astronauts. They don't need someone to point out their weaknesses. Rather they need someone to cheer them on to further victory through encouraging support.

So, if people don't change through the motivation that negative evaluations bring, then how do they change. A large part of the +P Certification Training, as you'll discover in section three, is designed to help IWs understand this very issue. We won't go into great detail here, but the basic idea comes from Titus 2:11-12.[9] In these verses, Paul points out that God's grace trains us to reject godless ways, worldly desires, and to live self-controlled, upright lives in this present age. It is God's grace that trains us to live godly lives; godliness does not come from trying to raise our score on an evaluation form.

This point seems very important to me as it relates to our discussion about the need for safety in the IW/MCP relationship. IWs need to talk about their most embarrassing and sensitive weaknesses. If God's grace is the agent He uses to train us to righteousness, it seems that a big part of any person involved in the change process in another's life needs to point them to God's bountiful grace that washes away their failures. If IWs feel uncomfortable talking about their struggles with their MCP, the MCP loses the opportunity to point them to God's grace and to thus be trained in living godly lives. SOs, therefore, would do well to try to provide their IWs serving in +P settings with some level of confidentiality in their relationship with the MCP, and to remove evaluative responsibilities from the MCP's role.

Trust Between the MCP and the Sending Organization

In the same way that it is important for the IW to be able to trust the MCP to provide a safe place to process struggles and failures, trust must be established between the MCP and the SO. The SO needs to know that if they give a measure of confidentiality between the MCP and the IW, this will not lead to the IW having secret ministry or team destroying policy violations or sins. The SO needs to trust that any problems an IW may have are being addressed appropriately and in way that takes into consideration employment laws and other legal considerations.

One salient example of this is the need for information a SO has when they determine that an IW should be terminated (e.g., if an IW commits a policy violation and is unwilling to address the inappropriate behaviors and needs to be sent home). Many employment laws that SOs are bound to follow, however, have strict requirements that must be met before an employee (in this case, an IW) can be terminated. In many cases, these require that the IW be given feedback about their performance deficiencies and opportunities to change before they are terminated. All of these steps need to be documented in the individual's personnel records. Often, MCPs are the ones who know the most about an IW's personal struggles and are in the best position to provide the documentation necessary to terminate an IW. SOs need to be able to trust that the MCP will help create the employment paper trail that is necessary for it to fulfill its legal employment mandates. If providing this type of information didn't change the relationship with the IWs they support, most MCPs would willingly do this.

When I served as a psychologist in the Air Force, we were also required to provide information to commanding officers about soldiers' fitness for duty - even though we knew this made it harder for the soldiers we were serving to trust us. Military mental health providers struggle to balance building trust with service members and providing their commanding officers with information important for them to make fitness for duty determinations. This conflict became clearest when I provided services to people who were working with nuclear weapons. The Air Force had a legitimate need to know if a person was unfit for working around weapon systems that could kill millions. However, this need to know put the service member in a difficult quandary; to get the help they needed meant that I was required to call their commanding officer and report to him or her that the service member was possibly unfit for duty - often resulting in a negative impact on their future careers. Obviously, service members were reluctant to disclose their true emotional state when they knew that it would be immediately reported to their commander who would then remove them from duty (and possibly not recommend them for promotion at the next promotion cycle).

In the last section, we discussed ways that trust between the MCP and IW can be created. These included the concept of normalizing problems and creating limited confidentiality in the IW/MCP relationship. Let's now turn to concrete ways that trust between the MCP and the SO can be facilitated.

Assurance that the MCP is Dealing with Important Issues: Limits to Confidentiality

The limits to a confidential relationship, outlined in the previous section, also serve the purpose of building trust between the MCP and the SO. The limits to the privacy offered to the IW are designed to provide assurance to the SO that the MCP will take appropriate actions when he or she discovers an issue that is potentially damaging to the SO or its ministry. This assurance that important issues the IW may have are being taken care of by the MCP, and that when appropriate, the MCP will provide appropriate SO leadership with information about the IWs situation, are the backbone to building trust between the MCP and the SO.

It may seem counter intuitive but having a measure of confidentiality in the relationship between the IW and the MCP will actually help the SO in its quest to prevent secret, ministry-destroying sins among its IWs. The most destructive thing for both an IW and SO is having an IW fall into some behavior that is too shameful to talk openly about with any representative of the SO. These behaviors then fester and grow into monsters that cause ministry death and destruction. Examples of such secret sins are prevalent in any SO's history. They range from IWs who leave their families to have an affair and marry a local individual, to IW's who are closet alcoholics, to those who secretly visit prostitutes. The effects of these secret sins damage the SO's relationship with their local partners, affect the morale of other IWs, create suspicion among the SO's financial supporters, and discredit the name of God and those who follow Him. As we have already discussed, IWs, due to stress-empowered flesh issues, are at higher risk for developing these destructive patterns. The best-case scenario for helping IWs not to fall into such sins is to intervene with them when they first fall into the temptation or behavior. Providing a safe place where the IW can discuss their weaknesses without feeling like it will cause them to be negatively evaluated by their SO leadership helps the SO avoid the very things that they do not want to happen.

Let me just give a brief example. By giving limited confidentiality and normalizing his struggles as stress related responses, I was able to develop a safe relationship with a young, married IW I supported a few years ago. When this man began to have feelings towards a local woman, rather than hide these feelings and try to deal with them on his own, he felt safe enough to tell me about these struggles and let me support him through the temptation. The risk that the SO took in giving me and this IW limited confidentiality actually paid off for them in that this young man was able to receive the support he needed to keep from falling into family and ministry-destroying sin.

In order to create an environment that is conducive to this kind of relationship, the SO needs to have some assurances that the MCP is actively dealing with issues like these when they come up. In addition, the SO needs some assurance that the MCP is keeping records that can help it meet the legal standards necessary if the IW engages in some behaviors that will eventually require termination from the SO. While SOs will have different legal requirements that they must adhere to (depending on which country or state they are registered in), some general principles for how MCPs deal with struggling IWs might be helpful.

Policy Violations

In the model that we've been discussing and working to create, the struggles that IWs have, including policy violations and discipline problems, are to be dealt with as stress reactions. Returning to our warfare analogy, struggles that IWs have are analogous to a soldier's battle wound. There is no shame in falling in battle. Battlefield injuries happen because the enemy attacks with the intent to kill. A soldier falls in battle because of the work of the enemy, not because of some weakness. Applying this analogy to IWs, their struggles and failures should be viewed as battle injuries. They fall not because of weakness, but since their enemy attacks them in their weak areas.

MCPs can be thought of as military medics. One of their primary jobs is to help injured soldiers get the aid that they need. They do this with compassion and grace, meeting the wounded IW with mercy and tenderly helping arrange the care that is needed for their recovery. The IW's job, in this case, is to receive the care that the MCP provides. **In a scenario like this, the only thing an IW can do "wrong" is to refuse the care that the MCP is trying to provide.** This would be analogous to the IW becoming a deserter in the military, not accepting the medic's help, and leaving the battlefield never to fight again. However, as long as the IW brings the "injury" into the relationship with the MCP, they do nothing wrong. Only if they would refuse the help of the MCP would they be considered needing some type of administrative intervention or discipline.

In the program I'm advocating, I make a distinction between a policy violation and, what I call, an *egregious* policy violation. In this model, a policy violation, a period of struggle or moral weakness, is akin to a battlefield injury; it happens because the enemy attacks the IW at their point of weakness. As long as the IW brings a policy violation into his or her relationship with their MCP, allowing the MCP to intervene and arrange whatever help is needed, then the IW's behavior is treated as a stress reaction and will not be used in administrative actions against the IW. An example of a policy violation like this would be an IW who struggles with pornography. If the IW brings this struggle into his or her relationship with the MCP, the MCP will treat it as a normal stress reaction and work to help the IW get whatever support is needed to overcome the struggle; the struggle would not be entered into his or her personnel record as an example of substandard performance.

An *egregious* policy violation, in this model, is analogous to a soldier who deserts from his or her unit. The message the soldier gives is that he or she doesn't want to change and doesn't want to receive help from the people who are wanting to provide support or care. Egregious policy violations, though also likely related to stress reactions, represent a complete collapse in the soldier's desire and ability to function appropriately. In a case like this, the only recourse his or her leader has is to initiate a court martial. An example of an IW's egregious policy violation would be a young man who has a sexual relationship with a local woman. If this young man, when confronted about the impropriety of this relationship, refuses to change his ways and says something to the effect of, "I don't care what anyone else thinks, I love this woman and I'm going to continue this relationship with her no matter what!" - this would be an egregious policy violation. The only thing that a SO and MCP can do in this situation is to separate the IW from service. If, however, the IW repents and asks for help from his MCP, then it would be considered a normal policy violation - a stress-empowered flesh issue, and the MCP would take whatever steps would be necessary to help the IW recover and return to healthy service.

In order to develop trust between the MCP and the SO in situations where a member is struggling, it is important that the MCP keep records of the IW's struggles and the ways that these are being addressed. This allows the SO to call on these records if they are ever needed to fulfill legal employment requirements. My suggestion, however, is that the MCP keep records like this in his or her own files, apart from the individual's official personnel records.

For example, in the case of the young man who is struggling with pornography, the MCP should keep records of the plan he or she implements to support the IW deal with his struggles. These records should be kept only in a secure file maintained by the MCP, and not entered into the employee's personnel records unless there is a future egregious policy violation. I refer to this type of record keeping as "In Desk Action Plans", meaning that they are kept in the desk of the MCP unless they are needed for some administrative action at a later date.

The rational for this type of record keeping also comes from my Air Force days. In the Air Force, at least when I was serving, it was not uncommon for a commander to keep what was referred to as an "in desk letter of counseling". This letter of counseling would list examples of deficient behavior, contained a plan for correcting the problem, and was signed by both the commander and the airman. It was not, however, entered into the airman's official records. The commander, rather, kept the letter in his or her desk. If the problem situation was resolved in the specified period of time, the commander would destroy the letter. However, if the airman had additional problems, or did not take the agreed upon steps to correct the problem, then the commander could bring the letter our from his or her desk and enter it into the personnel records. This method allowed the commander to address issues of concern without it necessarily hurting the soldier's future career advancement. If needed, however, the commander had appropriate documentation to start administrative proceedings against the soldier.

In the same way, I think that the MCP keeping action plans and "in-desk" documentation on the struggles and steps taken to ameliorate the issues that IW's have may serve to create trust both between the IW and the MCP, and the MCP and the SO.

Evaluations

Evaluations for IWs serving in +P areas should also reflect the program that we've been outlining. If IWs have been thoroughly screened to rule-out psychological problems, have demonstrated their motivation to deal with stress-empowered flesh issues by completing +P certification training, and are spiritually mature, then evaluations should serve a different purpose than in other settings. +P certified IWs don't need to be improved; they don't need their motivation increased; they are extremely motivated, talented and highly equipped for the tasks that they are doing. What IWs serving in +P setting need is support and encouragement as they do very difficult and stressful assignments, not suggestions and expectations that they will move their evaluation scores from a 3.5 to a 4.0. In extremely stressful environments, any hint of negative evaluation can quickly undermine spiritual and emotional morale, leaving the IW demoralized and questioning their ability to continue serving.

In the model that we've been developing, any issues that come up for IWs serving in +P settings should be attributed to stress. In this model, the purpose of evaluation is not to help the IW grow, but to encourage and support them. If the struggles that IWs face while serving overseas are analogous to combat injuries, then the only time a person would receive a negative evaluation is if they refused the help and support that they need. This would be classified as an egregious policy violation (see previous section), and termination would be indicated.

To create an environment where the negative effects of evaluation are minimized, I suggest that the typical evaluation form and procedure be revised. Many typical evaluation forms I have seen include scales where a person's performance on several work-related variables is rated on a 1 to 5 point rubric. Such rating scales are designed to show levels of performance as it relates to excellence, thus showing areas where improvement is needed and providing motivation or incentive for improving performance (i.e., "If you can't improve this area to a "3" by the next evaluation, we'll need to let you go.").

For IWs serving in +P settings, I suggest getting rid of the 1 to 5 point rating scale. I think these scales only serve to make IWs feel demoralized and increase their stress. +P IWs are highly motivated and making every effort to do their best. They don't need someone telling them that they are only 3.5 on a certain variable on a 5 point scale. The implied message is that this is not good enough.

The type of procedure I suggest for evaluations is to create minimum standards for each area related to IW service. For example, for the "Team Relationship" variable, the standard could be something like:

STANDARD: The IW participates in team life. He or she appropriately addresses team issues with a balance of humility and assertiveness. He or she actively addresses issues within him or herself that lead to team struggles. If there are temporary challenges in team functioning or relationship, the IW actively engages with his or her MCP to resolve these issues.

Standards like this would then be evaluated on a "Yes" or "No" basis, where SO leadership would decide if the IW is meeting the standard or not. As noted in the standard, if there are temporary challenges to team relationships, the IW is actively engaging with his or her MCP to resolve the issues. As long as any issues are being addressed with the support leader, the IW would meet the standard and get a positive evaluation. A negative evaluation would only be given for egregious policy violations, situations where the IW is having team troubles, but is not working with the MCP to address these issues. An egregious policy violation would necessitate that the IW be terminated from employment with the SO.

In addition to Team Relationships, other variables that I have included on evaluation forms include: Work Performance; Cross-Cultural Adjustment; Safe Conduct; Ministry; Soul Care; and Moral Conduct[10].

❊ 4 ❊

PUTTING IT ALL TOGETHER
WITH A CASE STUDY

Bill[1] is a 27-year-old single man who has served with his SO for two summers in a non +P setting. He has recently felt a call to leave his job in the States and go to serve full-time in a hazardous, +P setting with his organization.

Bill is well qualified professionally for the work he would be assigned to in the +P country. He comes well recommended from his previous employer, his pastor, and from the team leaders of the short-term summer teams he has served on in the past two years. From materials he submitted on his application and from the follow-up interview process, he seems to be a mature Christian with many talents. He also agrees with the SO's statement of faith and community covenant. Based on this information, Bill is accepted to serve with his SO.

However, before Bill is allowed to serve in a +P setting, he is informed that he will need to undergo psychological screening to make sure he is suitable for serving in a highly stressful area. He is also told that prior to his service in a +P country that, in addition to the normal training his SO sends IWs through, he will also need to complete a special +P certification training course.

Bill is given several psychological tests and is interviewed by a qualified psychologist. These tests and interview are designed to rule-out the presence of mental disorders (especially personality disorders) and fleshly vulnerabilities that would make him unsuitable for service in a hazardous country.

The psychological screening reveals that Bill has no current psychological diagnoses or conditions. When he was 14 years-old, however, he did go through a period of depression related to his parent's divorce. There was no history of suicide attempts or cutting behaviors, and his depression lifted after six sessions of counseling and eight months of time. He has not struggled with any other emotional issue (other than occasionally having periods where he feels blue or melancholic) since. He did, however, admit to an occasional battle with viewing sexual materials online. He reported that in the last several years he has had significant victory in this area, and with the help of his accountability group from church, has not viewed pornographic materials for over two years.

The psychologist and leadership committee feel that Bill is suitable for service in a +P setting and recommend him for the +P certification training course.

In early July, Bill completes all the normal orientation and training requirements that his SO has for all new IWs. In these courses, he learns how to adapt to a new culture, how to communicate the Gospel to people in his host country, tips for learning a foreign language, and the logistics of living overseas. He is also given basic expectation for team life, team conflict resolution strategies, and professional training for successfully accomplishing the work assignment he will be given. The emotional cycle of adjusting to a new culture was also presented, as was training in personal safety and computer communication protocols. Most of the cohort that Bill trains with leave for their assignment in non +P settings soon after they complete this orientation course. However, due to the added stressors of serving in +P context, Bill is required to complete +P Certification Training before he is allowed to start his assignment.

+P Certification Training is described to Bill as very intensive, like special forces training. It is to prepare and equip him for successful service in hostile areas. Successful completion will also allow his SO to support him in different ways while he is serving in his +P assignment. Successful completion will show his intent and willingness to deal with issues that can lead to personal and team failure. He will accomplish this by learning to die to self and put on spiritual armor at a deeper level. He and his teammates will be taught specific and concrete ways to do this during the training.

+P Certification Training is the beginning of an on-going process that will continue while he serves in his +P assignment. His MCP will support him in this process as he applies what he has learned in training to the real-life stress he will encounter during service.

+P certification training will also equip Bill for spiritual battle. It will help him see the "treasure of the Kingdom of God"[2] that he will willing, "with joy" sell all his fleshly passions to obtain. In certification training, Bill will be asked to examine his heart, mind and flesh in a new and deeper way so that he can be a "clean vessel" ready for the Master to use for good works.[3]

For the training, Bill is sent for two weeks to a +P country where a training center has been established. The first week of his training is designed to help him understand what stress is, and how spiritual factors can mediate his stress responses. Successful completion will require Bill to examine his automatic emotional responses and his flesh. Bill is told that what he is being asked to do is to die to his flesh in deeper ways, to purify his heart, and to deal with things that might cause team conflicts. Doing all this is very difficult. However, the training will be accomplished in a supportive and encouraging environment with trained staff to assist him. Bill is reminded that he is free to withdraw from training at any time and serve with his SO in a non +P setting. To serve in a +P country, however, he must complete the training.

In +P Certification Training, Bill and his teammates learn about stress, the additional stressors of serving overseas, the unique stress of being a Christian worker, and the stressors common in serving in hazardous, +P places. The relationship between stress, flesh, and spiritual warfare is taught, and a new model for dealing with flesh and stress is introduced.

In training, Bill learns that his past experiences influence his automatic emotional responses, which are unconscious and implicit. These responses can be equated with his flesh when they lead him to act or think in ways that separate him from God. Unless these automatic responses are consciously attended to and reprocessed, they easily become spiritual strongholds that the devil will use to empower his flesh and attack Bill, his ministry, and his team.

Bill learns the relationship between his thoughts and his automatic emotional responses. He learns that conscious thoughts can inhibit his automatic responses, and that faith is a conscious choice that can change emotional responses. Bill also learns that he can choose which thoughts he has because he is a spiritual being. His spiritual life gives him the power to choose to live in a way that is not dictated by his environment. Because he is a spiritual being, he can choose to "turn the other cheek,"[4] and he can have "contentment in every situation."[5] He learns that his emotional responses can be mediated and inhibited by his thoughts.

Bill learns that his heart is important because the passions that are in it determine what he will want. His heart directly affects which thoughts he chooses to have. From his heart, he will have desires to have God-pleasing thoughts or thoughts that will empower his flesh. Bill learns that one's heart cannot be changed with willpower. Willpower, rather, is defined as a powerful force that helps us to get what our heart desires. Willpower can't change a person's heart; the heart best changes through experiencing God's grace through faith.

Bill is instructed that successful service is empowered by walking in God's grace and he is taught new ways to experience and understand God's grace which is sufficient for whatever struggles the future holds. The battle with his flesh that Bill will experience in the highly stressful +P environment is something that cannot be won by self-effort. Rather, the battle should drive him into a deeper sense of God's great grace. This will fuel Bill's passion for God which will lead to his holiness.

Through the exercises in +P training, Bill learns that he still holds anger and bitterness towards his parents for their divorce. He learns how this will affect his team relationships and is supported as he uses the new model he has learned to deal with this by choosing to forgive his parents.

Bill also turns to God and receives forgiveness for an inappropriate relationship he had when he was 20. The grace he receives serves as a model for how he can treat his teammates, giving them grace when they struggle.

Bill learns what it will be like to come under spiritual attack while serving in a +P context. This is often a battle for the mind where the enemy uses failures, a sense of worthlessness, and lack of visible fruit to discourage IWs and empower their self-comforting flesh responses. Bill is taught that the struggles and failures he will experience in a +P setting are not due to lack of effort or because he is a failure as a Christian or IW. Rather, the struggles, failures and ineffectiveness that the devil wants to use to discourage him are normal parts of doing a very hard job in an extremely stressful situation. They can be thought of as battle wounds and can be approached without shame or fear.

During +P Certification Training, Bill and his team are taught the spiritual/emotional response model to dealing with stress. They are also provided with extra resiliency measures they can use in times of crisis. And finally, they receive training for how to prepare for the unlikely possibility of a very traumatic situation (e.g., kidnapping, assault, or terror attacks).

Once Bill and his team have passed their psychological screening, systematically dealt with underlying flesh issues, learned how to handle stress, gained a new understanding of stress-empowered spiritual battles, and have demonstrated a willingness to deal with issues that will hinder their service and relationship with God and team, they earn the title of being +P Certified.

The last step of Bill's preparation for overseas service is to complete his stress practicum and team bonding exercise. Bill and his cohort's assigned task is to learn the Arabic alphabet in a week's time, a possible but difficult task.

Before they begin studying the alphabet, however, Bill is assigned and introduced to his company's MCP, Scott. Scott is the one who will support Bill and his team as they serve in their new assignment in a +P context.

In preparation for the stress practicum and team bonding Scott Skypes with Bill and his cohort and explains that learning the Arabic alphabet will help them as they serve overseas, but that it is a difficult and frustrating task that will likely cause a lot of stress. Scott's role during the week will be to help them recognize their stress responses, and to help them apply the model they have just learned in +P Certification Training to the real-life stress they experience. Special emphasis will be given to team dynamics that will arise during the internship. These often include competition, envy, frustration, anger, and conflict.

During the internship week, Scott Skypes nightly with Bill and his team to process the stress that they noticed during the day's study. Scott reminds them of what they have just learned in the +P Certification Course and walks them through exercises that help them think about what is happening in their various emotional and spiritual response systems. He reminds them that the struggles they are feeling are normal stress reactions and he approaches them without shame or negative evaluation.

During the internship week, Scott frequently asks Bill and the others what support they need. He explains to them that this will be his primary role after they are deployed to their assignment, to monitor how they are doing and help arrange whatever support they need to do their job well. At the completion of the week, Bill is sent to his new +P assignment, and Scott and his team leader make sure to help him with the logistics of settling into his new life and work.

Once Bill settles into his new life, he begins sending his weekly Needs and Stress Inventory (NSI)[6] to Scott each Friday evening. On the NSI he describes his stress level related to several variables relevant to living overseas. Among others, these include his overall stress level, the security situation in his city/country, his mood, financial situation, the quality of team relationships and his health. Scott monitors his weekly reports and corresponds with Bill about any issues, needs or concerns that arise.

Bill's first three months go well, and his positive experience is reflected on his weekly NSI ratings. However, two weeks before Scott is scheduled to visit Bill and his team, Bill sends an NSI that reflects negative mood, team issues, and a moderate level of overall stress. Scott follows up on this by Skyping with Bill. He notes to Bill that his stress level is creeping up and that he notices team relationship is becoming an issue. Bill reports that he feels burned-out and exhausted from work and language study, and that he and his teammates seem on edge with each other.

Scott reminds Bill that these are normal reactions after living in stressful environment for this long. He reminds Bill of some of the strategies that he learned in +P Certification Training and they agree to talk about the situation more when Scott visits in a few days. Scott notices that Bill's teammates NSIs also reflect poor quality team interactions. At the same time he is communicating with Bill, he is also writing to the other teammates providing them with encouragement and support.

On the following week's NSI, Bill shows a slight decrease in both his overall stress level and team issues. However, his scores represent that he has struggled spiritually and with purity during the last week.

The following week, Scott visits Bill and his team for a planned visit. Scott meets individually with each team member and then with the whole team. In his individual meeting with Bill, he finds him discouraged since he feels he is ineffective with his ministry and work and isn't a very good language learner. He feels that the local people hold him at a distance and don't seem very interested in having any kind of relationship with him. In addition, he has struggled with "lust issues" and admitted that in a moment of weakness he looked at web sites that he shouldn't have.

Scott supportively listens. He reminds Bill that struggles like this are not because he is a bad person, unmotivated, or failing as a Christian or IW. Rather, they come from the difficulty of the job he is doing in the heart of enemy territory. The enemy is surely attacking him and trying to empower his flesh through stress.

Scott also reminds Bill of what was covered in the +P Certification training - that God's grace is what empowers ministry. The struggles Bill has should point him to experience God's grace in new ways and fuel his passion and love for God. This love will help change his heart and give him more power over fleshly struggles.

Scott also helps Bill identify thought patterns that the devil uses to trap him in the fleshly way of dealing with the stress he is experiencing. Scott and Bill also look for automatic emotional responses that might be related to Bill's stress load. Scott prays for Bill and asks God to empower him spiritually so that he experiences God's love and pleasure for him in new ways. He reminds him that God takes pleasure in him[7] even in the midst of his struggles and encourages him to spend more time each day just enjoying God's love for him as a sinful, imperfect man.

Scott asks Bill if it is OK if he keeps a few notes about their interaction in a private and secure file on his computer. He assures Bill that, as per their SO's limited confidentiality agreement, their discussion will remain confidential and that none of what they have talked about will be entered into Bill's personnel files. The notes are just for Scott to use to pray for him and to check up on him later.

The confidentiality that Scott offers, as well as the way he approaches the struggles as stress-related battle wounds, helps Bill trust Scott and the system set in place to support him. Bill feels that he has relative safety talking about even embarrassing issues with Scott and that it won't affect his standing with his sending organization. Shame about his struggles is minimized by Scott emphasizing that changes come through grace and not by trying harder.

During his visit, Scott also explores the team issues. After meeting individually with each team member and supporting them in much the same way he has Bill, he calls a team meeting. During the team meeting, Scott notes the sense of disunity that the team is struggling with. He reminds them that this is normal in highly stressful settings and is usually related to flesh issues that they all bring into the team relationship. The team stress gives each of them an opportunity to examine their hearts in a deeper way, learn to forgive each other, die to self, practice accepting each other, and extending grace the way that God does to each of them individually. Scott reminds the team that the issues they are facing are not due to any underlying mental health issues (these were all screened out), and that team relationship is a top priority that they need to protect from the enemy's attack. During times of stress and attack, it is easy for team-mates to become angry with each other and turn against each other when what is really needed is to turn towards each other. The team is reminded that they can control their team relationships through choosing to forgive, by loving each other as imperfect people, and by dying to self.

Three weeks after his visit, Bill sends Scott another NSI that shows high stress, spiritual and purity issues. Scott calls Bill and supportively listens as Bill describes that his "lust issues" feel out of control. Scott arranges for Bill to fly to the country where he resides (which is nearby and not an expensive flight) and spend a weekend with him to discuss this issue in more depth.

During the time together, Bill describes that his struggles with internet usage have gotten worse and, try as he may, he feels they are out of control. He is worried he might be addicted to pornography and feels great shame for being an IW who fails so miserably. He is worried that his behaviors are so bad that his SO leadership will send him home as a "moral failure" for treatment.

Scott thanks Bill for being willing to trust him enough to talk about this issue that brings him so much shame. He reminds him that, though pornography use violates the standards of their SO, since he has brought this to the attention of Scott and seeks his help, it will remain confidential between the two of them and not be entered into his personnel records. It is important for Bill to be willing to continue to work with Scott on this issue, however.

Scott, again, frames Bill's struggles as stress-empowered flesh issues that happen under stress and spiritual attack. He reminds Bill that, like he learned in +P certification, he needs to bring this into his relation-ship with God; God's grace is sufficient for even this. The long-term power to deal with the fleshly vulnerability associated with this struggle will come from the heart change that results when Bill accepts God's grace and love for him at deeper levels.

Scott suggests to Bill that they create an Action Plan for this issue. The action plan will be kept in a secure file on Scott's computer and not be entered into Bill's personnel file as long as Bill continues to work with Scott on this issue. The action plan, which both Bill and Scott sign, notes that Bill is feeling shame and guilt for using pornography under times of stress, and that he is working with Scott to receive the support he needs to deal with this policy violation.

Bill is given the following actions to complete:

1.) He is to actively work to accept God's forgiveness for this area.

2.) He is to fight against the identity issues that the devil tries to use in these struggles and continue to view himself as a child of God that struggles with flesh.

3.) He is to examine what the enemy and God are trying to accomplish through this struggle.

4.) He is given the name of a Christian counselor in the city where he lives that he is encouraged to go to for support.

5.) He will seek support from other men as they fight this battle together.

Bill returns to his assignment feeling supported in his struggles, excited about God's grace, willing to keep Scott informed of his issues, and excited to tell people the Good News of God's love for broken and sinful people. In the coming weeks, Scott continues to monitor Bill's completion of the Action Plan and his overall ratings on the NSI. Though not perfect, Scott makes good progress and actively works on the action plan. His weekly NSI ratings continue to decrease as he learns to walk in God's grace.

At their next scheduled evaluation session, Scott's evaluation reflects that Bill is meeting all the standards of the SO. This is despite the fact that pornography use is against the SO's code of conduct. Since Bill is actively engaging with Scott to resolve this issue, it is treated as a stress reaction. Bill is not treated as someone who is deficient, but rather as someone whose intense stress level has led him to struggle with a fleshly weakness. Scott's goal is to help Bill receive whatever support he needs to resolve this stress-empowered flesh issues, not to correct him into better performance.

* * *

Interested readers are invited to continue in the ***Effective Kingdom Service in Hostile Places*** series. Book one describes in detail the intense stress that international workers, especially those serving in hostile places, experience, and how this stress makes them vulnerable to fleshly weakness. Book three walks the reader through the Special Forces Training for the Soul, a program designed to build Godly resilience by experiencing anew God's grace and love in ways that will transform the heart and mind and protect it from stress-empowered flesh issues.

APPENDIX ONE
THE NEEDS AND STRESS INVENTORY (NSI)

The Needs and Stress Inventory is a simple Excel worksheet that IWs in +P settings fill out each week and send to their Support Leader (SL). It takes about three minutes to complete. The SL uses the information in the weekly NSI to better understand in which areas the IW is struggling so that appropriate support can be provided. One organization I consulted with allowed the SL to send a $10 Amazon gift card for every four NSIs that an IW completed, which helped with compliance.

Here is a sample NSI record. Below this form is the descriptors that automatically popup when the mouse hovers over each of the 10 rated variables on the Excel worksheet.

Weekly Needs and Stress Inventory (NSI)

NAME: **Sample IW**

DATE: **Today**

How are things going this week in each of the following areas? INSTRUCTIONS: Please provide a quick but thoughtful rating of each of these variables. Your ratings should be according to a -10 to +10 point scale, where negative numbers refer to more negative feelings or state of affairs, zero is neutral, and positive numbers represent an increasingly positive feeling or state of affairs. Please note: Your ratings will only be reviewed by your SL who will use them to arrange support and encouaragement for you. They will NOT be included in your personnel records.

TEAM	-2
MOOD	-4
FINANCES	5
SAFETY/SECURITY	6
WORK ASSIGNMENT	1
WALK/SOUL CARE	3
PHYSICAL HEALTH	-2
PURITY	-2
HOME COUNTRY ISSUES	5
(MARRIAGE/FAMILY)	2

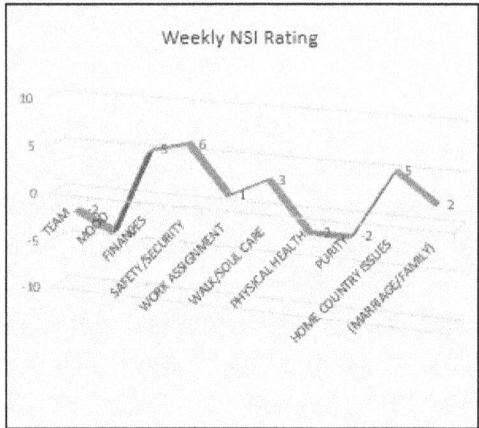

Weekly NSI Rating

Now, in the box labeld TOTAL STRESS below, please provide a 0 to 10 rating of your overall stress level for this week. On this scale, zero represents a minimal stress level and 10 represents an extreme stress level.

TOTAL STRESS	4

TOTAL STRESS

VARIABLE DESCRIPTIONS:

Team: The quality of your team relationship and functionality for the week.

Mood: How was your overall mood this week?

Finances: Negative numbers represent increasing financial stress. Positive numbers represent and increasingly good financial situation.

Safety/Security: Positive number represent an increasingly good security situation, whereas negative numbers represent increasing stress related to real or perceived threats.

Work Assignment: How pleasant (or unpleasant) and productive was your work assignment this week?

Walk/Soul Care: Negative numbers represent spiritual dryness, lack of fruit, and/or lack of closeness to the Father. Positive numbers represent a sense of closeness to the Father, opportunities, and/or fruit.

Physical Health: Positive numbers indicate health, energy and vitality. Negative numbers indicate physical illness, accidents, injuries or physical and emotional exhaustion.

Purity: Negative numbers represent perceived struggles, level of temptation or perceived failures. Positive numbers indicate a sense of victory over a previous area of struggle. Zero represents no struggles and no perceived temptations.

Home Country Issues: Note the effects of news from home, either good or bad.

(Marriage/Family): For married couples and families, please rate the quality of your marriage and family relationship this week. Singles, leave this blank.

APPENDIX TWO
A SAMPLE EVALUATION FORM

Name: _____ **Dates of Evaluation Period:** _____

Support Leader: _____**Date of Evaluation:**_____

Country or Service: _____ **Work Assignment:**_____

Does the member meet the standards of performance as described below for each of the following areas? If the standards are not met, give specific examples of how they are not met and the plan for ameliorating the deficiency. Both the employee and the Support Leader should review and sign the document when completed.

WORK ASSIGMENT

STANDARD: Professionally and diligently performs work assignment to the glory of the Father. If there are temporary challenges in performing work assignments, the employee actively engages with his or her Support Leader to resolve these issues.

Does this person's conduct meet this standard?

Yes ( )

No ( )

If standard not met, please give specific examples below, using additional pages as necessary:

1.

2.

3.

If standard not met, please list specific ways that this person will work to ameliorate the problem:

1.

2.

3.

TEAM

STANDARD: Participates in team life. Appropriately addresses team issues with a balance of humility and assertiveness. Actively addresses issues within him or herself that lead to team struggles. If there are temporary challenges in team functioning or relationship, the employee actively engages with his or her Support Leader to resolve these issues.

Does this person's conduct meet this standard?

Yes ( )

No ( )

If standard not met, please give specific examples below, using additional pages as necessary:

1.

2.

3.

If standard not met, please list specific ways that this person will work to ameliorate the problem:

1.

2.

3.

CULTURE

STANDARD: Appropriately engages the local culture. Is sensitive to and respects cultural differences. Studies the local language as possible. If there are temporary challenges in appropriately behaving in the local cultural context, the employee actively engages with his or her Support Leader to resolve these issues.

Does this person's conduct meet this standard?

Yes ( )

No ( )

If standard not met, please give specific examples below, using additional pages as necessary:

1.

2.

3.

If standard not met, please list specific ways that this person will work to ameliorate the problem:

1.

2.

3.

SAFE CONDUCT

STANDARD: Adheres to the organization's recommendations for safe conduct. Makes reasonable efforts to ensure personal safety. If there are temporary challenges in adhering to standards of safe conduct, the employee actively engages with his or her Support Leader to resolve these issues.

Does this person's conduct meet this standard?

Yes ()

No ()

If standard not met, please give specific examples below, using additional pages as necessary:

1.

2.

3.

If standard not met, please list specific ways that this person will work to ameliorate the problem:

1.

2.

3.

OUTREACH

STANDARD: Thoughtfully and appropriately engages in outreach activities. Adheres to organizational guidelines. If there are temporary challenges in the way CR is conducted, the employee actively engages with his or her Support Leader to resolve these issues.

Does this person's conduct meet this standard?

Yes ( )

No ( )

If standard not met, please give specific examples below, using additional pages as necessary:

1.

2.

3.

If standard not met, please list specific ways that this person will work to ameliorate the problem:

1.

2.

3.

SOUL CARE

STANDARD: Takes active steps to nurture and protect his or her spiritual life. Engages in appropriate community activities. Works to promote the spiritual life and growth of teammates. If there are temporary challenges in the way that soul care is accomplished, the employee actively engages with his or her Support Leader to resolve these issues.

Does this person's conduct meet this standard?

Yes ( )

No ( )

If standard not met, please give specific examples below, using additional pages as necessary:

1.

2.

3.

If standard not met, please list specific ways that this person will work to ameliorate the problem:

1.

2.

3.

MORAL CONDUCT

STANDARD: Adheres to the organization's code of moral conduct. If there are temporary challenges in adhering to the organization's code of conduct, the employee actively engages with his or her Support Leader to resolve these issues.

Does this person's conduct meet this standard?

Yes ( )

No ( )

If standard not met, please give specific examples below, using additional pages as necessary:

1.

2.

3.

If standard not met, please list specific ways that this person will work to ameliorate the problem:

1.

2.

3.

I have reviewed this evaluation and understand that within 72 hours I can submit written comments to my Support Leader. My comments and this evaluation form will then be entered into my official personnel records.

_____

Name:

_____

Signed:Date:

_____

Support Leader's Name:

_____

Signed:Date:

NOTES

PREFACE

1. *War Psychiatry: Combat Stress Casualties; Disorders of Frustration and Loneliness, PTSD, Army, Navy, USAF Psychiatry, Postcombat Reentry, Traumatic Brain Injury, PSTD, Prisoners of War, NBC Casualties (Emergency War Surgery Series).* 21st Century Textbooks of Military Medicine, Progressive Management. Kindle Edition.
2. Eye Movement Desensitization and Reprocessing (EMDR) is a scientifically validated treatment of Posttraumatic Stress Disorder (PTSD). For more information on EMDR see the EMDR web page at www.emdr.org.
3. Titus 2:12 (NET)

1. MEMBER CARE IN +P SETTINGS

1. O'Brian, D. (2009). *In the Heat of Battle: A History of Those Who Rose to the Occasion and Those Who Didn't.* Oxford, Osprey Publishing, p. 9.
2. Corbett, S., and Fikkert, B. (2009). *When Helping Hurts: How to Alleviate Poverty Without Hurting the Poor....or Yourself.* Moody Publishers, Chicago.
3. See II Cor 12:1-10, for example. Also see the section in Chapter 6 of the first volume in this series titled "The Thorn Law".
4. "Do not take gold, silver, or copper in your belts, no bag for the journey, or an extra tunic, or sandals or staff, for the worker deserves his provisions." Matt 10:9-10 (NET)
5. The Mayo Clinic has a good general overview of personality disorders on their web page: https://www.mayoclinic.org/diseases-conditions/personality-disorders/symptoms-causes/syc-20354463. Accessed 01/21/2020.
6. C.f., General, Surgeon. *21st Century Textbooks of Military Medicine - War Psychiatry: Combat Stress, Postcombat Reentry, Traumatic Brain Injury, PTSD, Prisoners of War, NBC Casualties (Emergency War Surgery Series). Progressive Management.* Kindle Edition.
7. C.f., Siegel, *Handbook of Interpersonal Neurobiology.*
8. c.f., https://www.parinc.com/Products/Pkey/464
9. https://www.cdc.gov/violenceprevention/acestudy/index.html
10. https://www.npr.org/sections/health-shots/2015/03/02/387007941/take-the-ace-quiz-and-learn-what-it-does-and-doesnt-mean
11. c.f., 1 John 5:17

2. PRE-FIELD TRAINING

1. *War Psychiatry (Emergency War Surgery Series).* 21st Century Textbooks of Military Medicine, Progressive Management. Kindle Edition, Loc. 25
2. The "low road" will be described in volume three of this series.

3. "For the grace of God has appeared, bringing salvation to all people. It trains us to reject godless ways and worldly desires and to live self-controlled, upright, and godly lives in the present age...." Titus 2:11-12 (NET)

4. *War Psychiatry*, Kindle Location 310

3. CREATING TRUST

1. Siegel. *Pocket Guide to Interpersonal Neurobiology*. p. 76
2. John 8:3-11
3. "There is no fear in love, but perfect love drives out fear, because fear has to do with punishment. The one who fears punishment has not been perfected in love." 1 Jn 4:18 (NET)
4. There are other good reasons to not use the term "member care" in +P countries. One important consideration is the term member care and MCP is exclusively used by missionary organizations; secular organizations use terms like "personnel office" or "employee assistance". The term member care is easily searched on the internet and can identify people who call themselves as MCPs to be supporting missionary work. This could easily put the IWs that they are trying to support in a compromising situation.
5. WhatsApp is messaging program that is popular in many +P countries and, due to its option to send encrypted messages, is commonly used by SOs to communicate with their IWs.
6. Please contact the author directly for information on how to obtain and use this inventory.
7. 1 Thessalonians 4:1 (NET)
8. "Now on the topic of brotherly love you have no need for anyone to write you, for you yourselves are taught by God to love one another. And indeed you are practicing it toward all the brothers and sisters in all of Macedonia. But we urge you, brothers and sisters, to do so more and more...." 1 Ths 4:9-10 (NET)
9. "For the grace of God has appeared, bringing salvation to all people. It trains us to reject godless ways and worldly desires and to live self-controlled, upright, and godly lives in the present age,...." Titus 2:11-12 (NET)
10. Appendix Two includes a sample evaluation form for individuals serving in +p settings.

4. PUTTING IT ALL TOGETHER WITH A CASE STUDY

1. This is a fictitious case study. The incidents described in it are common, though.
2. "The kingdom of heaven is like a treasure, hidden in a field, that a person found and hid. Then because of joy he went and sold all that he had and bought that field." Matt 13:44 (NET)
3. "Now in a wealthy home there are not only gold and silver vessels, but also ones made of wood and of clay, and some are for honorable use, but others for ignoble use. So if someone cleanses himself of such behavior, he will be a vessel for honor-

able use, set apart, useful for the Master, prepared for every good work." 2 Tim 2:20-21 (NET)

4. "But I say to you, do not resist the evildoer. But whoever strikes you on the right cheek, turn the other to him as well." Matt 5:39 (NET)

5. "I am not saying this because I am in need, for I have learned to be content in any circumstance. I have experienced times of need and times of abundance. In any and every circumstance I have learned the secret of contentment, whether I go satisfied or hungry, have plenty or nothing. I am able to do all things through the one who strengthens me." Phil 4:11-13 (NET)

6. A sample NSI is available in Appendix One.

7. "The Lord your God is in your midst; he is a warrior who can deliver. He takes great delight in you; he renews you by his love; he shouts for joy over you." Zeph 3:17 (NET)